A QCS Mark for the
Irish Public Service

CPMR Research Report
4

A QCS Mark for the Irish Public Service

Peter C. Humphreys
Michelle Butler
Orla O'Donnell

IPA
INSTITUTE OF PUBLIC
ADMINISTRATION

First published in 2001
by the Institute of Public Administration
57-61 Lansdowne Road
Dublin 4
Ireland
in association with
The Committee for Public Management Research

www.ipa.ie

British Library Cataloguing in Publication Data
A catalogue record for this book is available from the British
Library.

ISBN 1 902448 54 5
ISSN 1393-9424

Cover design by M. and J. Graphics Ltd.
Typeset by the Institute of Public Administration
Printed by ColourBooks Ltd, Dublin

CONTENTS

Executive Summary

CHAPTER 1: Introduction
1.1 Previous CPMR research findings
1.2 QCS research: next phase
1.3 Accrediting QCS in the Irish public service
1.4 Agreed terms of reference
1.5 Research approach
1.6 Report content

CHAPTER 2: Defining Quality Customer Service
2.1 Introduction
2.2 What does quality mean?
    2.2.1 Product quality
    2.2.2 Quality and performance
2.3 Delivering public services
    2.3.1 Types of public service
    2.3.2 Quality in a public service context
    2.3.3 Who is being served?
    2.3.4 Refocusing public services on the citizen
    2.3.5 Citizen participation
2.4 A working definition of quality
2.5 Managing quality
2.6 The importance of quality accreditation
2.7 Concluding remarks

CHAPTER 3: Quality Accreditation in an International Context
3.1 International overview
3.2 Cross-national accreditation frameworks
    3.2.1 ISO 9000
    3.2.2 EFQM Excellence Model
    3.2.3 Speyer Quality Approach
    3.2.4 The Common Assessment Framework (CAF)
    3.2.5 Malcolm Baldrige National Quality Award (MBNQA)
3.3 Approaches adopted in individual countries
    3.3.1 Australia
    3.3.2 Canada
    3.3.3 Denmark
    3.3.4 Finland
    3.3.5 New Zealand

3.3.6   United Kingdom
3.3.7   United States of America (USA)
3.4   Concluding remarks

CHAPTER 4: Irish Policy Background
4.1   Introduction
4.2   Strategic Management Initiative (SMI)
4.3   Building blocks
4.4   The QCS Initiative (1997)
4.5   Customer Service Action Plans (1997-2000)
4.6   Challenges to be addressed (2001-2004)
4.7   QCS Working Group (1999 onwards)
4.8   Programme for Prosperity and Fairness (PPF)
4.9   Developments in the wider public service
4.10 Involvement with existing quality
       accreditation schemes
       4.10.1 ISO 9000
       4.10.2 The Q-Mark
4.11 Concluding remarks

**CHAPTER 5:   Developing a Quality Accreditation
                        Framework**
5.1   Introduction
5.2   High-level accreditation frameworks
       5.2.1   Leadership
       5.2.2   Strategy and planning
       5.2.3   People
       5.2.4   Organisational management
       5.2.5   Processes
       5.2.6   Customer
       5.2.7   Civic responsibilities
       5.2.8   Overview of high-level frameworks
5.3   Supportive frameworks
       5.3.1   Investors in People
5.4   Towards a framework for accreditation
       in the Irish public services
       5.4.1   Building a customer focus
       5.4.2   Processes
       5.4.3   Customer results
5.5   The way forward

CHAPTER 6: A QCS Mark for the Irish Public Service
6.1   Introduction
6.2   Some key management challenges

6.3 International experiences
6.4 Potential evaluation criteria
6.5 A QCS mark for the Irish public service:
     an outline scheme
     6.5.1 *Levels of achievement*
     6.5.2 *Frequency/duration of award*
     6.5.3 *Level of eligibility*
     6.5.4 *Coverage*
     6.5.5 *Prestige of award*
     6.5.6 *Process*
     6.5.7 *Assessment criteria*
     6.5.8 *Assessment examples*
     6.5.9 *Funding*
     6.5.10 *Management and administration*
     6.5.11 *Going forward*
6.6 Concluding remarks

Notes and References

Appendix 1: Revised Quality Customer Service
             (QCS) Principles for Customer
             Action Plans (2001-2004)

Appendix 2: Investors in People National Standard

Appendix 3: Examples of quality standards used
             in the UK by central government
             departments, executive agencies and
             local government

Appendix 4: Exploring concepts of quality in other
             public sector approaches: The Canadian
             Public Service

Executive Summary

Research background

The Committee for Public Management Research (CPMR) was established in 1997 to develop a comprehensive programme of research to serve the needs of future development in the Irish public service (http://www.irlgov.ie/cpmr). As part of this remit, the CPMR has undertaken a series of major studies to inform the development of a Quality Customer Service (QCS) approach in the civil and wider public service. The study was undertaken during the period April-December 2000 by research staff from the Institute of Public Administration.

Drawing upon previous research, this current study focuses on the critically important issues of accreditation and recognition. In particular, by critically evaluating current arrangements, and drawing upon best practice here and elsewhere, this study provides objective and practical suggestions as to how best to introduce a QCS Mark in the Irish public service.

This study was also undertaken in consultation with the QCS Working Group which has a vital role to play in taking forward the current QCS Initiative in the civil and wider public service.

Why research a possible QCS Mark for the Irish public service?

At the planning stage of the research, initial consultations indicated that:

- There is considerable support for the view that the development of an effective service-wide system of accreditation and recognition (i.e. a QCS Mark) could have a key role to play in the next phase of the QCS Initiative.
- A well-designed QCS Mark scheme could assist the internal and external promotion of a quality customer service, by raising awareness and morale, and acting as a driver for progressive change.
- Such a development could also have major implications for the promotion of a benchmarking approach to QCS by the public service.
- It could provide a platform to facilitate the sharing of best practice among organisations, promote healthy competition and allow achievement to be acknowledged.

- An appropriate and effective QCS Mark scheme could also facilitate improved service delivery integration within and between public bodies.

Scope of the research

Accordingly, this study seeks to:

- review current quality accreditation systems in Ireland and elsewhere. This will help identify the range of approaches available, potential key elements and appropriate concepts for an Irish public service QCS Mark system

- identify (a) the potential benefits and other implications for the Irish public service from the introduction of a voluntary and attainable QCS Mark system and (b) the key issues to be addressed in order to introduce system-wide accreditation

- outline a framework for QCS accreditation in the Irish public service and how such a system might be administered and resourced

- make recommendations on the steps to be taken to introduce the proposed system, in the civil service in the first instance, with a view to its extension to the wider public service.

Our research presents:

- a detailed review and evaluation of relevant QCS and quality management literature. This has helped us to identify key issues and to develop an appropriate conceptual framework upon which to design a QCS Mark for the public service

- an analysis and evaluation of relevant international material on existing accreditation schemes and effective national or federal approaches to the development and implementation of such schemes

- in-depth discussions with key personnel in government departments, external agencies, commercial organisations and trades unions, as well as a cross-section of public service providers in order to obtain evaluative feedback on existing and potential future arrangements.

Report content

Following an introductory chapter which outlines the rationale and terms of reference for the research:

- *Chapter Two* draws upon current national and international thinking to explore what exactly is meant by 'Quality Customer Service' within a public service and in the wider context. A working definition of quality for the purpose of this research is identified as: *the extent to which service delivery and/or service outcomes meet with the informed expectations and defined needs of the customer.*

- *Chapter Three* contains detailed information on relevant QCS initiatives internationally and on the systems in use in Australia, New Zealand, Canada, the UK and the USA. Cross-national examples include the ISO 9000 series, the European Foundation for Quality Management (EFQM) model and the Malcolm Baldrige National Quality Award.

- *Chapter Four* plots the main developments to date regarding QCS in the Irish public service and establishes the policy context within which the proposed QCS Mark would be taken forward.

- *Chapter Five*, drawing upon the information on international and national developments, identifies and develops an appropriate conceptual framework for Ireland.

- *Chapter Six* proposes an appropriate approach to QCS accreditation in the Irish public service and suggests the next steps that could be taken.

Key management challenges

Quality accreditation has a central role to play in developing a total quality approach to quality management in the civil and public services. Our research findings indicate that achievement of quality requires that a number of significant challenges are addressed. These challenges include:

- the promotion and acceptance of quality customer service as one of the key principles of public service delivery. To achieve this, quality needs to be an integral part of services and to be seen as the responsibility of everyone involved in the design and delivery of services

- visible and effective leadership at the most senior level, together with the championing of quality customer service values throughout the organisation and its business processes
- the development, design and delivery of services in a manner which is genuinely customer-focused and responsive to changing customer needs and expectations
- effective management of the complex relationship between the customer and the range of other stakeholders (including the staff, the taxpayer and elected representatives) to minimise conflicts of interests in terms of what is understood as quality customer service
- a focus on the customer, with citizen participation in the design and delivery of services. Real participation will require customer and citizen involvement to move beyond consultation towards the promotion of partnership and negotiation between all stakeholders.

Challenges relate also to the nature of public services, their diversity and complexity, and to the fact that roles, responsibilities, functions and budgets are externally imposed upon public service organisations. Nonetheless, responsibility for the design and delivery of quality services rests primarily with the organisation.

It is also abundantly clear to us that addressing these challenges will raise issues that strike at the heart of an organisation's mission and purpose.

Outline scheme
We conclude that there is a compelling case for introducing an award scheme to recognise excellence in quality customer service in the Irish public service. Such a scheme should be designed to honour excellence and pre-eminence in the field of public service delivery and have a distinctive national identify and branding. However, given the current early stage of development of many Irish public service bodies in their adoption of quality management approaches to the delivery of services, we also suggest that a new QCS Mark scheme should be voluntary in character, simple but meaningful, challenging but also attainable. Its administration would have to be robustly objective and fair.

While representing a prestigious achievement within itself, a new QCS Mark for the Irish public service should also provide an opportunity for organisations to progress towards a higher level, internationally recognised, framework such as the EFQM.

Based upon these findings, together with a review of the current position in Ireland, we outline an appropriate framework for the introduction of a QCS mark for the Irish public service which includes specific suggestions regarding:

- recognition of different levels of achievement (including bronze, silver and gold awards)
- frequency/duration of the award, as well as the obligations of award winners
- level of eligibility (i.e. individual business units/teams of staff providing specific goods or services primarily to external customers)
- geographical coverage
- award profile
- accreditation process
- assessment criteria (i.e. quality standards, equality/ diversity, physical access, information, timeliness/ courtesy, complaints, appeals, consultation/evaluation, choice, official languages equality, better co-ordination, internal customer, leadership, strategy/planning and investment in people)
- assessment examples
- funding
- management/administration.

Assuming that a QCS scheme is approved in due course, further detailed development work would be necessary to ensure that the administrative and support structures would be in place to allow the initial self-assessment phase and first applications to be received at the earliest opportunity.

Study conclusions

We acknowledge that a QCS Mark for the Irish public service could not aspire to, nor could it practically seek to, address all the current challenges faced by public service bodies in their efforts to mainstream customer service values throughout their organisations and business processes. It should certainly not be seen nor promoted as a panacea for present shortcomings. However, our research shows that such a scheme could make a very significant contribution to taking the next phase of the QCS Initiative forward in a meaningful way. Above all, if properly introduced and managed, it could result in significant improvements in the quality of services provided to the public, as well as significant improvements in the recognition and morale of those providing those services.

There are champions of quality customer service in the Irish public service, in all sectors and at all levels of staff in many organisations. Such champions have little recognition, formal or otherwise, of the vital work they do. A well-designed QCS mark scheme could both provide a means of acknowledging that achievement, encouraging its far greater development, and provide a valuable tool for organisations of all sizes to embark upon a meaningful programme of continuous quality improvement.

CHAPTER 1

Introduction

1.1 Previous CPMR research findings

The Committee for Public Management Research (CPMR) was established in 1997 to develop a comprehensive programme of research to serve the needs of future development in the Irish public service. As an early priority, the CPMR initiated a series of major studies to inform the development of a Quality Customer Service (QCS) approach in the civil and wider public service. In the first of these studies, Humphreys (1998) concluded that, '... with some notable and noteworthy exceptions ... there is still a very long way to go before it can be asserted that Irish public service organisations have taken on board wholeheartedly the need to be customer-focused throughout the design, planning, implementation, monitoring, evaluation and review of the services delivered ... Rarely were customer needs placed centre stage (CPMR Discussion Paper No. 7, p.77)'.

Humphreys (1998) also concluded that '...it is important to attempt to plot possible ways forward which will encourage rather than discourage those positive tendencies already developing within the Irish public service. It will also be important to facilitate the sharing of experience across the public service of constructive approaches to addressing customer service needs within a realistic management context (CPMR Discussion Paper No. 7, p.78)'. With these objectives in mind, the CPMR undertook a detailed assessment study of best practice approaches to the mainstreaming of customer service values in its Discussion Paper No. 11 (1999). This research included a detailed assessment of the significant progress made to date, from a QCS perspective, in the Department of Social, Community and Family Affairs and in Meath County Council (see Humphreys, Fleming and O'Donnell, 1999).

1.2 QCS research: next phase

When launching the latest phase of the Strategic Management Initiative (SMI) at Dublin Castle, *Delivering Quality Public Service – Responding to the Changing Environment* (Aherne, 1999), the Taoiseach outlined the next steps for improving the quality of services provided by the state to the public (see Chapter Four). Those steps included the re-establishment of a Quality Customer Service Working Group (QCSWG). This group comprises representatives from departments/offices across the civil service, as well as representatives of the private, community and voluntary sectors and independent expertise[1].

The terms of reference for the QCS Working Group are:

- to monitor and evaluate progress at the level of departments/offices across the civil service
- to develop mechanisms for sharing experiences and good practice at the level of departments/offices and across the civil service
- to oversee the development of mechanisms for benchmarking and for recognising improvements in quality service delivery
- to develop better internal customer service focus in order to drive external customer service in tandem with the business planning process.

To facilitate its work, the working group has formed three sub-groups to inform its thinking in the areas of benchmarking, best practice and equality/diversity. Under the leadership of the Chairman of the Board of Revenue Commissioners, and reporting to the SMI Implementation Group, the QCSWG has a key role to play in taking forward the next phase of this important programme. Given this role, it was clearly desirable to develop the present study in consultation with the QCS Working Group.

1.3 Accrediting QCS in the Irish public service

Drawing upon research already undertaken by the CPMR and elsewhere (see References), and following consultations with the QCSWG and its sub-groups, this study focuses on the critically important issues of accreditation and recognition. There were a number of reasons for this:

- There is considerable support for the view that the development of an effective service-wide system of accreditation and recognition (i.e. a QCS Mark) could have a key role to play in the next phase of the QCS Initiative.
- A well-designed QCS Mark Scheme could assist the internal and external promotion of a quality customer service, by raising awareness and morale, and acting as a driver for progressive change.
- Such a development could also have major implications for the promotion of a benchmarking approach to QCS by the public service.
- It could provide a platform to facilitate the sharing of best practice among organisations, promote healthy competition and allow achievement to be acknowledged.
- An appropriate and effective QCS Mark scheme could also facilitate improved service delivery integration within and between public bodies.

By critically evaluating current arrangements, and drawing upon best practice here and elsewhere, our research seeks to provide objective and practical proposals on how best to introduce a QCS Mark in the Irish public service[2].

1.4 Agreed terms of reference

Accordingly, the following terms of reference were agreed by the CPMR. The study would:

- review current quality accreditation systems in Ireland and elsewhere to identify the range of approaches available and potential key elements and appropriate concepts for an Irish public service QCS Mark system
- identify (a) the potential benefits and other implications for the Irish public service from the introduction of a voluntary and attainable QCS Mark system and (b) the key issues to be addressed in order to introduce system-wide accreditation
- outline a framework for QCS accreditation in the Irish public service and how such a system might be administered and resourced

- make recommendations on the steps to be taken to introduce the proposed system, in the civil service in the first instance, with a view to its extension to the wider public service.

Commencing in April 2000, it was agreed that a final draft report would be completed in November 2000. This timetable would facilitate the use of the research findings in taking the next stage of the QCS Initiative forward through the QCS Working Group.

1.5 Research approach

In order to deliver effectively on these agreed terms of reference, our research has:

- a detailed review and evaluation of relevant QCS and quality management literature. This helped us to identify key issues and to develop an appropriate conceptual framework upon which to design a QCS Mark for the public service
- an analysis and evaluation of relevant international material on existing accreditation schemes and effective national or federal approaches to the development and implementation of accreditation schemes
- in-depth discussions with key personnel in government departments, external agencies, commercial organisations and trades unions, as well as a cross-section of public service providers in order to obtain evaluative feedback on existing and potential future arrangements.

1.6 Report content

Following this introductory section, *Chapter Two* draws upon current national and international thinking in order to explore what exactly is meant by 'Quality Customer Service' within a public service, and in the wider context. *Chapter Three* contains detailed information on relevant QCS initiatives internationally. *Chapter Four* plots the main developments to date regarding QCS in the Irish public service, and establishes the policy context within which the proposed QCS Mark would be taken forward. In addition to documentary analysis, this chapter draws upon detailed feedback from in-depth discussions with key actors in the areas of service accreditation, the SMI QCS Initiative, service providers and social partners.

Chapter Five, drawing upon the information on international and national developments, identifies and develops an appropriate conceptual framework for Ireland. Finally, drawing upon information gathered at each stage of the research, *Chapter Six* proposes an appropriate approach to QCS accreditation in the Irish public service and suggests the next steps that could be taken to introduce such a system. A full list of references is provided and detailed supporting evidence is presented in the notes and appendices.

CHAPTER 2

Defining Quality Customer Service

2.1 Introduction

At the outset, it is vital to understand what is meant by the term 'quality customer service' (QCS) and how it can be promoted and managed effectively. The purpose of this chapter is to explore concepts of 'quality', 'quality customer service' and 'effective quality management'. By drawing upon the numerous debates in the literature about quality and quality management, this chapter serves primarily to:

- highlight some of the key themes in these debates
- set QCS accreditation within the wider context of quality management
- highlight some of the key issues that relate specifically to public service provision.

Each of these issues is addressed in turn.

2.2 What does quality mean?

There is little doubt that 'quality' is a concept that is difficult to define. Most people relate to quality but often have difficulty describing it (see Pounder, 2000). In fact, quality often goes unnoticed until it is absent. One of the reasons for such definitional difficulty is that quality means different things to different people, depending upon their personal experiences, expectations and needs. As a consequence, customers may perceive the same service in different ways. Edvardsson (1998) argues that it is '...the customer's total perception of the outcome which is 'the service' and that what they do not perceive does not exist'. Similar issues are also addressed by Townsend and Gebhart (1986), and Groth and Dye (1999). Such a situation suggests that, however quality is defined, those involved in the design and delivery of quality goods and services need to ensure that the service criteria are consistent with the expectations of customers. Similarly, there is a need to consider differences arising from the nature of the product or service provided and the quality of its provision.

2.2.1 Product quality

Quality can be defined as the degree to which a product meets with the relevant technical specifications, where the emphasis is on zero defects and reducing the degree of variation between products, i.e. quality control. In such circumstances, compliance with procedures and retrospective inspection is a key feature. This concept of quality is frequently used in manufacturing but even there rapid changes in product requirements can be problematic (see Walsh, 1991). In addition, a product may conform perfectly with specifications but still prove useless to the end user.

Within the public sector, a more useful concept of quality is 'fitness for purpose'. A product or service is fit for purpose if it meets with the purpose for which it is intended. This concept is more useful for our purposes because it is more related to the provision of services than goods, but yet it may still fail to make an explicit connection with the needs of the customer. There remains an unanswered question. Who decides the purpose for which a service is intended, the providers or the end users? Public services need not only to be fit for specification and fit for purpose, they need to meet the qualitative and quantitative needs of users and potential users.

Milakovich (1992) outlines three sources of quality in service organisations. They include:

- *hardware* – structures and equipment, which are tangible sources measured in the same way that products would be measured e.g. a broken bed in a hotel or a faulty transformer in an electric utility

- *software* – procedures and processes – although often seen as intangible sources, software sources may be the most important of all

- *humanware* – personnel – the element of services unique to an employee, such as customer relations.

Milakovich (1992) points out that it is often believed that service quality is composed entirely of humanware but, in fact '...the degree of service quality experienced by a customer results from the combination of all three sources, each providing legitimate areas to measure and improve (p. 580)'; (see also Kano and Gitlow, 1988-89). As Boyle (1989) has also pointed out, quality can be seen as performance, from the customer's perspective.

2.2.2   Quality and performance

Overall, two main aspects of performance relating to quality are identified in the literature:

- appropriateness, effectiveness, and consistency, i.e. doing the right thing right every time

- fairness in the delivery of services, i.e. equity in the distribution/accessibility of services to all users and potential users.

These underpin service delivery and relate to the potential of services to meet user expectations. However, as already indicated, the satisfaction of users with services will depend, in part at least, on the qualitative experience at the user/service interface, as determined by the 'hardware', the 'software' and the 'humanware' (see Milakovich, 1992).

The link between performance and quality is particularly strong in the health literature. As Shaw (1986) points out, quality involves far more than just consumer satisfaction. It includes appropriateness, equity, accessibility, effectiveness, acceptability and efficiency. Within the health context for example, the key issue in quality is not concepts of customer satisfaction, such as acceptability, but appropriateness. Shaw illustrates this: '... suppose that following a confusion of histology reports a patient undergoes an unnecessary operation. The ward may be comfortable, the staff may be skilled and attentive, the procedure meticulously performed, no complications occur and comfortable discharge is carefully organised with the community care team. Nonetheless, if the procedure or service is inappropriate it cannot be 'good' (p. 11)'.

Overetveit (1991) helps to clarify further the relationship between quality and performance by identifying three types of quality:

- *client quality*: what consumers want from the service
- *professional quality*: whether the service meets needs as defined by professional providers and whether it correctly carries out techniques and procedures which are believed to be necessary to meet client needs
- *management quality*: whether the most efficient and productive use is made of resources to meet client needs, within limits and directives set by higher authorities/purchasers.

Referring to this conceptual model, Curry and Herbert (1998) suggest that:

- customer satisfaction measures and techniques ensure client quality
- standard setting and organisational audit ensure professional quality
- quality management is concerned with the development of an holistic approach that internalises the values and competencies of a quality approach in the system.

2.3 Delivering public services

Our discussion here has not focussed specifically on issues distinctive to provision by public bodies. Yet, as Humphreys (1998) has pointed out, there are important distinctions between the commercial and non-commercial sectors regarding the relationship between service provider and the customer. Shand and Arnberg (1996) observe that, in public service delivery, concepts of quality vary between OECD countries, reflecting differences in values and in relationships between providers and users. Such differences will reflect cultural and political differences and whether public service providers have a monopoly on providing services or operate in a competitive or market environment.

2.3.1 Types of public service

Dewhurst et al (1999) argue that the '...aim of a public

(service) organisation is to satisfy certain needs of a society, within the constraints of available budgets...' and that, although the needs and requirements to be satisfied are set externally, the way in which they are met is the responsibility of the public organisation itself. Potter (1988) suggests that there are broadly two kinds of public services:

- those that give people access to services that they would otherwise not enjoy

- those concerned with social control.

Nonetheless, the nature of services provided by public services today is diverse and complex, both in functional and organisational terms. Such functions include: giving or receiving payment, advice and information; providing entire services such as education, health or transport; and law enforcement and tax collection (see Shand and Arnberg, 1996). However, whatever the nature of the public service concerned, a central focus on quality in the design and delivery of public services is imperative.

2.3.2 Quality in a public service context

Shand and Arnberg (1996) have noted that focusing on quality reinforces the concept of public service ethos and they acknowledge that the very existence of public sector organisations is premised upon the delivery of a service or product to the public. Both Stewart and Clark (1987) and Claver et al (1999) go further and emphasise the central importance of the citizen/customer in public service organisations. They identify the following key features of quality public service provision:

- tasks and activities that are carried out are solely aimed at serving citizens usefully

- the organisation is judged according to the quality of the service given within the resources available

- the service offered will be underpinned by values which are shared by members of the organisation and citizens

- a high quality service is sought, i.e.

- prompt service is provided by all members of a section or department, and
- the problems that arise in public service delivery are thoroughly addressed

- there is a real relationship with the citizen, i.e.
  - there is frequent and meaningful contact with citizens, and
  - citizens are treated with respect and dignity.

Claver et al (1999) point out that such a citizen-focused approach represents quite a different and contrasting kind of corporate culture to that often found in public administrations, where traditionally: the management style is authoritarian; there is little internal or external communication; individuals have little scope for initiative; decision making is centralised and repetitive; and beliefs are conservative and reluctant to change.

Public services also often operate as monopolies, where users do not have the option of going elsewhere and continued subscription to services by the user may not therefore be an indication of satisfaction. Public services are delivered within limited resources and trade-offs may be required between meeting the needs and expectations of users and efficiency. In addition, demand for services may outstrip supply, impacting on access to services and the ability of providers to deliver services to standards that they themselves would value (see Humphreys, 1998). Potter (1988) identifies a particular paradox relating to the provision of public services. 'On the one hand, the nature of public services suggests they are of the utmost importance to those consumers who want to use them; on the other hand, the interests of individual consumers must constantly be juggled against the interests of the community as a whole, and of other groups who make up the community.'

2.3.3 Who is being served?
In the literature, quality service is often expressed in terms of 'customer focus' and 'customer satisfaction'. Customer focus relates to how services are designed to meet the requirements of the customer. This requires clarity about

who is the customer and what are the customers' needs. Customer focus also demands that the design of processes and working arrangements ensure flexibility and responsiveness to customer needs. As Gaster (1999) points out, quality is not 'one size fits all'. Customer satisfaction relates to how services are actually experienced and how services meet or exceed the expectations of the customer.

However, Humphreys (1998) has pointed out the limitations of the use of the term 'customer' given that most public services are normally delivered free of direct charge by monopolistic providers. Yet 'customer service' is the concept most generally used in the Irish context (see Chapter Four). The alternative term of 'client' is also not without the unfortunate, hierarchical connotations of professionals knowing better than those using their services (see Humphreys, 1998). In contrast, the term 'citizen' implies mutual rights and responsibilities in the provider-user relationship.

Donnelly (1999) explores further the relationship between the citizen and the customer in public services. One tension identified concerns the relationship between who pays and who uses services. 'The nature of many public services is such that there is collective or community payment for services which are not always enjoyed personally by every paying citizen. Conversely, there are some services where the individual receiving the service does not pay directly, or at all, for the service. In this context one might argue that citizens should have all the rights of customers receiving services along with additional rights of access – access to information, to influence and to debate around service and design (Donnelly, 1999)'.

Arrangements for funding, which often include direct and/or indirect subsidisation, can cause confusion over who the providers of services are accountable to. The distinction and relationship between the customer/citizen and other stakeholders in determining the needs and expectations of service users is also complex. Donnelly (1999) suggests that the complex character of public services means that some stakeholders may be excluded from services and/or be non-users of the services; they may be unaware that they are in receipt of services, and there may be stakeholders with directly conflicting interests. Humphreys (1998) differentiates between the 'consumer' (user) as one whose interest in the product or service provided shapes the service relationship, and the 'customer' where the service relationship is shaped by experience of using that service.

Another example of difficulty in defining who is the customer can be found in areas such as law enforcement where simultaneously there may be many customers – the victim, the offender, members of the community, the courts, the taxpayer and so on. Relationships between customers and providers of services are often considerably more complex than those found between customers and providers in the private sector. 'In public administration it has often been the case that the provision of the service to the public has not been that of a supplier to a customer but rather that of an *authority to a subject* ... public employees have found themselves primarily *as agents of the state* carrying out an official state purpose, rather than service personnel involved in the provision of a defined service to a customer (see Bendall, Boulter and Kelly, 1994, p.9).'

2.3.4 Refocusing public services on the citizen
In the resurgence of interest in quality in public services, much of the debate is focused on the relationship between the state and the citizen. Shand and Arnberg (1996) found in their review of quality initiatives across OECD countries that the thinking behind quality reforms was based on:

- resolving an inherent conflict between public servants and citizens in favour of citizens and shifting power from the supplier to the client
- basing the state's legitimacy on socially useful activity
- improving equality and democracy by recognising all clients (citizens) as having equal entitlements and thus obviating favouritism or corruption in the delivery of services
- administrative simplification or de-bureaucratisation

- market mechanisms and client choice being an integral part of client focus

- participation in decision making to improve the quality of services, particularly in local government.

Potter (1988) argues that in the delivery of public services a shift to the consumer is needed in the balance of power. She also explores the difficulties in applying the five principles of consumerism – *access, choice, information, redress,* and *representation* – to public services. In this regard, it is interesting to note the close correlation between these principles and those used by the Irish civil service in the first phase of its Quality Customer Service Initiative (see Chapter Four).

The particular difficulties that Potter identifies regarding *access* are, firstly, that the person using the service may not be the person paying for it, and so access cannot be translated into an automatic consumer right. Secondly, the decision about who should have access, and to what, is a political responsibility. The consumerist response to these issues would be to have clear criteria, open to public scrutiny, on which to base decisions. Another approach is to improve accessibility and to identify and remove the barriers to access.

Potter does acknowledge that consumer *choice* is limited in public services and suggests that often there are more pressing priorities in the delivery of public services, for example the redistribution of costs and benefits within society. In some services the issue of choice may not seem relevant at all. She suggests that popular views that public representatives are elected to make choices for the public is only valid if they are fully informed about the needs and wants of consumers. Two approaches that she cites to address the issue of consumer choice in public services are, firstly, to incorporate consumer views into performance measurement. Secondly, the notion of individual rights can be developed.

In terms of *information,* Potter suggests that information takes on an even greater importance in relation to public services. The services at stake are likely to be crucial to consumers' welfare and there is often a wide gap between information possessed by providers and consumers. Consumers need to be able to make the best choices about how to derive maximum benefit from the services available to them and to have general information on how services are run. She suggests that information relating to design of services, the decision-making processes and about rights to services, can confer real power on consumers in terms of their ability to influence change. In terms of *redress*, Potter stresses the importance to consumers of mechanisms to settle grievances quickly, simply and fairly and also claims that redress mechanisms bring wider benefits because they are a form of quality control.

Potter argues that *representation* is one of the more problematic principles of consumerism in public services. Issues relate to how the views of consumers can be adequately represented in all decisions concerning their interests. At the individual level, efforts to develop representation can include the development of advocacy for particularly vulnerable groups or the establishment of publicly funded bodies to represent consumers. The role of elected representatives is once again relevant in this area, especially in terms of how their decisions are informed by the views of consumers.

2.3.5 Citizen participation

Shand and Arnberg (1996) suggest that the components of responsive public service first identified by the OECD in 1987 – transparency, client participation, satisfying client requirements and accessibility – are still valid. Accordingly they have restated these values as follows.

- Clients participate in, or are consulted about, decisions on the level and type of service to be provided.
- They are informed as to the level and type of services to be provided.
- They can reasonably expect to receive this level of service.
- They have rights of complaint and redress if the appropriate level of service is not provided.
- Service delivery agencies are required to set quality targets and to report their performance against them.

There is however an inherent tension between seeking input from customers and delivering services that meet customer expectations. By explicitly focusing services on the needs of customers, it is likely that customer expectations of services will be raised. Failing to meet these expectations will then be perceived as a quality failure, even though services in effect may actually have been improved. In addition, in actively seeking the views of customers on quality, for example by setting up a complaints procedure which will result in an increase in complaints, issues about poor quality are made explicit. As such, at least initially, an increase in the number of complaints is not an indicator of diminishing quality of services.

Nonetheless, citizen/customer participation and empowerment is a vital component of developing customer-focused services. Edvardsson (1998) argues that customers are co-producers of services and their part in the process of service delivery affects results in terms of added value and quality. The implications of this view are far-reaching and the role, participation and responsibility of the customer must therefore be made clear.

Another issue that needs to be addressed here is the need to clarify what is meant by participation. This issue is the source of numerous debates in the literature and beyond the remit of this study to explore in detail. However, Arnstein's 'ladder of citizen participation', although over thirty years old, is still relevant today. It differentiates between three categories of apparent citizen participation in terms of the degrees of citizen power that they represent (see Figure 2.1). In fact, only one category represents true citizen empowerment.

Ham (1980) outlines four types of public participation:

- *negotiation* – a group's views are sought and the decision is contingent on that group's approval
- *consultation* – a group's views are actively sought and may or may not be taken into account
- *public relations* – a group's views are sought but in such a way as to rule out their influence over decision-making

Figure 2.1: The ladder of citizen participation

Citizen control Delegated power Partnership	Degrees of citizen power
Placation Consultation Informing	Degrees of tokenism
Therapy Manipulation	Non-participation

Source: Arnstein (1969)

- *articulation* – a group presents views without their views being sought.

This suggests that, if the aim of seeking input from citizens on the design and delivery of services is to develop services that meet with their expectations, relationships need to be built towards facilitating and promoting real partnership and meaningful negotiation. Edvardsson (1998) also argues that the expectations of customers need to be balanced with those of employers and owners and that there is no reason why quality improvement cannot be 'regarded as a game where all the participants are winners'.

2.4 A working definition of quality
We have outlined a number of concepts of quality and the relationship between providers and users in quality service. Gaster (1999) suggests that definitions of quality have to be negotiated and that there will be trade-offs between elements that are more or less important to different stakeholders. However, for the purposes of this study it is necessary to articulate a working definition of quality to inform our research process.

Based on a review of quality concepts, Boyle (1996) suggests that in terms of quality of service:

- it is the needs of users or customers and their specification of quality that is paramount when determining dimensions of quality

- the quality of the product, service delivery and the quality of the outcome of that product or service, in terms of its suitability to purpose, are important aspects of quality.

Given the preceding discussion, we choose the following definition of quality for the purpose of our research:

> *The extent to which service delivery and/or service outcomes meet with the informed expectations and defined needs of the customer*

This definition is helpful because it positions quality within the context of public service delivery and the relationship between public service organisations and the customer.

2.5 Managing quality

A clear concept of quality management is needed in order to inform and monitor the development of quality services.

A range of terms such as 'quality assurance' (QA), 'total quality management' (TQM), and 'continuous quality improvement' (CQI) is used to describe approaches to quality management. QA describes quality management perhaps in its broadest sense – ensuring that services and products meet with standards. The terms TQM and CQI are often used interchangeably. However, there are subtle differences between the two concepts.

The emphasis in TQM is on building a quality culture so that everyone is working to the same quality agenda. For example, ' ... improving the business, its internal and external relationships, its routines and methods of operation ... demands a culture where all aspects of the organisation are harmonised in the continuous pursuit of the organisation's mission and meeting the requirements of customers, shareholders, employees and the community (Bywater, 1991)'. According to Milakovich (1992) the TQM approach has been shown to reduce waste and duplication, increase efficiency, decrease costs, increase productivity and result in customer satisfaction.

The emphasis in CQI is on continuous assessment of an organisation's efforts to monitor and improve the quality of services and an ongoing evaluation to ensure satisfactory outcomes. In this sense, CQI helps to address a common criticism of quality approaches, that quality reviews are retrospective rather than continuous. Another criticism is that quality improvement – like consumerism – benefits the middle-class consumer most, neglecting wider social groups. Leahy (1998) suggests that the CQI approach may address such fears because it examines processes for all and therefore benefits all current (and potential) users of the service. Differences in traditional and modern concepts of quality management are illustrated in Figure 2.2.

Figure 2.2: Concepts of quality management

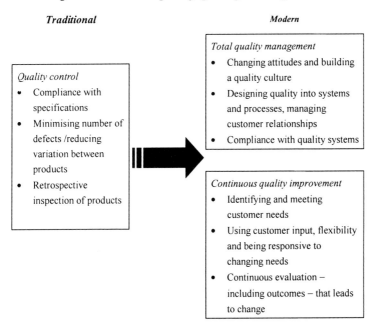

In this regard, it should be no surprise that, given its manufacturing origins, the emphasis in the traditional approach is on controlling quality, reducing variation between products and retrospective inspection. However, for the reasons given above, a proactive and dynamic approach is required to develop customer-focused and responsive public services. Accordingly, TQM or CQI are more appropriate approaches to building quality public services.

2.6 The importance of quality accreditation

Quality accreditation has a very important role to play in modern approaches to quality management by:

- making explicit agreed understandings of quality and by ensuring that all stakeholders – employers, employees, customers, citizens – know what to aim for and have feasible expectations of services. By making them explicit, understandings of quality are also set out for negotiation and realignment

- providing organisations with a focus for their efforts to improve services continuously. Once the key components of quality service are agreed, organisations can use information to review their own performance continuously, highlighting areas where they are performing well and priorities for improvement

- providing the means for benchmarking service, processes, outputs and outcomes and therefore identifying priorities for improvement. Benchmarking also enables good identified practice to be shared by organisations, further adding quality to services

- providing incentives for quality improvement and identifying organisations that are not making progress.

As will be seen in the analysis of current provisions in Ireland in Chapter Four, quality accreditation schemes could have a vital role to play in the voluntary promotion of change and improved management practice.

2.7 Concluding remarks

The purpose of this chapter has been to explore concepts of quality, quality customer service, public service delivery and quality accreditation within the context of effective quality management. Some key points emerge from this discussion.

- Quality customer service needs to be promoted and accepted as one of the key principles of public service delivery. As such, quality needs to be designed into services and to be seen as the responsibility of everyone involved in the design and delivery of services.

- Key challenges in developing quality public services relate to designing and delivering services that are customer-focused and responsive to changing customer needs and expectations.

- Challenges also relate to the relationship between the customer and the range of other stakeholders in public services. This needs to be appreciated and account must be taken of the potential for conflicts of interests in terms of what is understood as quality customer service.

- Challenges relate also to the nature of public services, their diversity and complexity, and to the fact that roles, responsibilities, functions and budgets are externally imposed upon public service organisations. Nonetheless, responsibility for the design and delivery of quality services rests primarily with the organisation.

- Quality customer service relates essentially to how services are perceived by customers and how experiences relate to expectations. Services need to be refocused on the customer and this will require citizen participation in the design and delivery of services. Real participation will require customer and citizen involvement to move beyond consultation towards the promotion of partnership and negotiation between all stakeholders.

- A working definition of quality for the purpose of this research is

  The extent to which service delivery and/or service outcomes meet with the informed expectations and defined needs of the customer.

- Quality accreditation has a central role to play in developing a total quality approach to quality management in the civil and public services.

Having established some of the key issues that need to be considered in the development of a planned and meaningful approach to the provision of quality services by public bodies, it is now important to review developments internationally, both cross-nationally and within individual countries (see Chapter Three).

CHAPTER 3

Quality Accreditation in an International Context

3.1 International overview

The majority of OECD countries began implementing quality policies in their public services in the mid to late 1980s. An OECD study (1996) observed that some countries focused on specific, high-profile initiatives or reforms of service quality (e.g. Belgium, Canada, France, Portugal, Spain, the United Kingdom) and that in others, like Ireland, it has been an ongoing and implicit aspect of wider initiatives (see Chapter Four). In some countries the OECD found that individual agencies were drawn together into a centrally promoted and co-ordinated initiative (e.g. Australia, Denmark, Finland, Norway and Sweden). Up to 1996, the latest stage of reform in OECD countries focused on citizen-centred government and noted that the use of quality accreditation schemes was the most prevalent form of quality management in the public service.

An international comparison of public service quality accreditation systems highlights the fact that there is no one 'best way' in quality accreditation, but a diversity of approaches. Here, we examine cross-national systems of accreditation and national systems which have often been developed within a wider cross-national framework. In summary, our objective is:

- to examine the range of approaches to accreditation undertaken in other countries with a view to providing an appropriate framework for an Irish scheme
- to provide an analysis and brief summary of the overarching concepts and elements of accreditation schemes.

3.2 Cross-national accreditation frameworks

We identified five different but inter-related schemes which are potentially relevant to the development of a QCS Mark for the Irish public service. These are:

- the ISO 9000 series
- the European Foundation for Quality Management (EFQM) excellence model
- the Speyer Quality approach
- the Common Assessment Framework (CAF)
- the Malcolm Baldrige National Quality framework.

Because of their international importance, each of these needs to be considered in turn.

3.2.1   ISO 9000

In 1987, the first international standards on quality assurance were published, known as the ISO 9000 series (see Rothery, 1996). As Figure 3.1 indicates, the ISO 9000 series is multifaceted, including ISO 9004 (Part 2) which aims to achieve a service standard by controlling the processes that deliver the service. The ISO series originated in defence procurement, evolved gradually into the manufacturing industry, and then to the services sectior, private and public. The European Union (EU) formally adopted ISO at the end of 1992. ISO is the international standard for *quality systems* which provides a basis for assessing an organisation, or part thereof, against objective requirements.

The standard requires that management show, define and document its policy and objectives for, and its commitment to, quality (see Bendell et al, 1994). Rothery (1996) sees the introduction of the services standard as significant, representing a major evolution of international attitudes towards the measurement of quality in the service sector and a brave attempt at introducing quantification to the service quality area, hitherto regarded as somewhat sacrosant and unquantifiable. ISO can be used for self-assessment or, following self-assessment, organisations can apply for registration through a national or European accreditation agency.

In Ireland, the National Standards Authority of Ireland (NSAI) is responsible for the ISO 9000 series and also provides consultancy for small and medium-sized enterprises (SMEs) to achieve accreditation (see Chapter

Figure 3.1: Overview of the ISO 9000 series

ISO 8402	Vocabulary
ISO 9004	Quality management Quality system elements
ISO 9000	Guidelines for selection and use of the standards

ISO 9001	ISO 9002	ISO 9003	ISO 9004 Part 2
Model for design/ development, production, installation and servicing.	Model for production and installation	Model for final inspection and test	The services standard

Four). ISO 9000 quality focus is on meeting pre-set criteria rather than on the performance required of the organisation or customer needs and expectations (see Seddon, 1997). ISO 9000 is being revised to seek to address these issues.

3.2.2   EFQM Excellence Model

The European Foundation for Quality Management's mission is to be the driving force for sustainable excellence in organisations in Europe. In 1991 the European Quality Award scheme was launched, which was developed in conjunction with the European Organisation for Quality (EOQ) with the support of the European Commission. EFQM adopted the Excellence model formally in 1996 with the objective of providing '...a model that ideally represents the business excellence philosophy and can be applied in practice to all organisations irrespective of country, size, sector or stage along their journey to excellence' (see Chapter Two). A model development manager was appointed in 1997 and, following benchmarking with other award models from around the world and consultations with all the EFQM Excellence Model's stakeholders, a new improved model was launched in April 1999 (see Figure 3.2).

Figure 3.2: EFQM Excellence Model

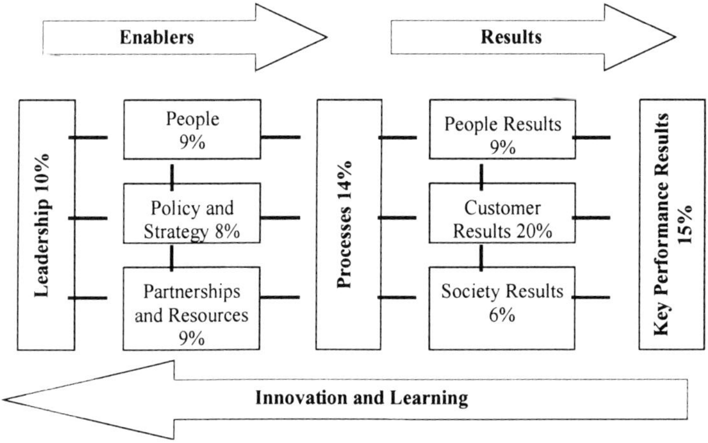

The 1999 model evaluates an organisation using nine performance criteria; comprising five 'enablers' (covering what an organisation does) and four 'results' (what an organisation achieves). 'RADAR is the essential business logic at the heart of the model determining the success of the quest for performance improvements' (EFQM, 1999f). The acronym RADAR encapsulates five elements: Results, Approach, Deployment, Assessment and Review.

The EFQM Excellence Model is generic: it applies to business and 'non-business' orientated organisations (such as government departments and agencies and non-profit organisations). However, EFQM has published a public and voluntary sector version of the model, which reflects the differences that exist between different types of organisations and between countries. For example in the

United Kingdom (UK), the focus of public sector quality is on customer orientation, whereas in Germany public sector quality concentrates on administrative modernisation and innovation. The criteria for the public and voluntary sector version of the EFQM Excellence Model involve changes to policy and strategy, people, processes, customer results, and key performance results. The public and voluntary sector version inserts 'owning stakeholders' instead of shareholders and includes 'comparators' as well as competitors to reflect a lack of competition in areas of the public sector.

The EFQM Excellence Model '...recognises there are many approaches to achieving sustainable excellence in organisations' and therefore, '...can respect and subsume work being undertaken with other models, systems and procedures, e.g. Balanced Scoreboard, Customer Value Chain, Investors in People (UK), Charter Mark (UK), the Speyer Award (Germany, Austria, Switzerland), New Public Management, ISO Certification and country specific quality assurance and certification systems'. Excellence Ireland is the EFQM's national partner in Ireland (see Chapter Four). Large and small organisations, commercial and non-commercial, may apply to become members. Members' annual subscriptions range from euro 1,000 to 10,000, dependent upon size of the organisation and type of membership (e.g. associate, general).

The EFQM Excellence Model offers two awards: the European Quality Award and the European Quality Prize. The European Quality Prize is presented to individual public sector organisations and small to medium-sized enterprises (SMEs). The European Quality Award is presented to the best of the winners. Using the Prize or the Award logo adds prestige to products and services. Each year the winning organisations are invited to share their experience with others in a series of conferences throughout Europe (see EFQM, 1999b).

3.2.3 Speyer Quality Approach

The German National School of Public Administration in Speyer established a Quality Award scheme in 1992. This public sector award is organised every two years by the school and primarily involves German, Austrian and Swiss public service organisations. The Fifth Speyer Quality Award 2000 is awarded for the successful modernisation of public administrations and the competition applies to the whole public sector, i.e. federal, state and local administrations, including public enterprises and associations. A key stipulation for applicant organisations is that they must be 'a separate organisational unit with a degree of autonomy and independence'. Registration for applicants costs DM 750.

The Fifth Speyer Quality Award 2000 focuses on six central themes:

- citizen/client focus
- e-government
- human resource management
- politics and administration
- public private partnership and knowledge management.

Application for the Speyer Quality Award is on a self-assessment basis. Self-assessment enables public administrations to scrutinise their organisations and, through project groups, to modernise them. A self-assessment form, plus supporting documentation, is normally completed by applicants and submitted to the National School of Public Administration by May of the year concerned. Applications are evaluated by a group of experts during June to August and site visits conducted during September. Evaluation of organisations focuses on specific areas:

- coherence of objectives
- quality of concepts elaborated
- how concepts are put into practice
- innovation
- quality of project management
- usefulness and transferability of experience in other contexts.

The prize committee meets in November and selects award winners. The awards ceremony takes place in December. Benchmarking with other administrations, and information exchange during the congress at the end of the competition, motivates organisations to further improve their administration.

The Speyer Quality Award is supported financially by sponsoring partners (e.g. commercial banks, assurance companies, consultants, software companies). It seeks to create innovation coalitions with its sponsoring partners and continuously integrates modern management and quality concepts (from the private and the public sphere, the national and international level) into the model. The Speyer Quality Award is presented every two years to public sector organisations who have successfully modernised their administrations.

3.2.4   The Common Assessment Framework (CAF)

Although of very recent origin and of much smaller scale than other European frameworks, the Common Assessment Framework (CAF) seeks to blend key elements from both the EFQM and Speyer approaches. It is the result of collaboration between member states under successive EU presidencies (UK and Austria in 1998, Germany and Finland in 1999 and Portugal in 2000). The CAF is essentially an aid to public administrations in the EU to understand and to introduce the use of quality management techniques in public administration. The main purpose of CAF is to provide a simple, easy-to-use framework which is suitable for self-assessment of public sector organisations. As such, it is very much a 'light' framework. It is acknowledged that any organisation undertaking a more fundamental programme of analysis and development would choose a more developed quality management model. The CAF does, however, offer the opportunity for meaningful introduction to more comprehensive approaches to quality management within the public service.

Similar in approach to the EFQM, the CAF focuses on nine criteria:

- leadership
- policy and strategy

- human resource management
- external partnerships and resources
- process and change management
- customer/citizen-oriented results
- people (employees) results
- impact on society
- key performance results.

CAF provides a self-assessment framework, under which a representative group of employees in an organisation can perform a critical assessment of their organisation. This self-assessment procedure is less rigorous and less detailed than an organisational assessment conducted by trained external assessors. The self-assessment result depends totally on the accuracy and frankness of the assessor(s). Each of the assessors must be able to explain and justify their answer to an external assessor, by reference to evidence of actual structures, activities or results of their organisations. To date, the CAF has been pilot-tested on a small number of organisations with varying degrees of exposure to quality management at central, regional and local levels of public administration. This procedure is also much less expensive, and has some advantages such as revealing the perceptions of staff towards their own organisation. It also provides the opportunity for benchmarking across the EU. Initially launched during the Portuguese EU Presidency in May 2000, uptake and evaluation of the CAF is continuing.

3.2.5 Malcolm Baldrige National Quality Award (MBNQA)

This award scheme was established by the US Congress in 1987, under the Malcolm Baldrige National Quality Improvement Act, '...to recognise US organisations for their achievements in quality and business performance and to raise awareness about the importance of quality and performance excellence as a competitive edge'. In fact, the Baldrige Award was developed by the US government as a result of the poor performance of American products relative to the quality of Japanese products during the

1970s.   The US government developed an award package that would draw attention to American organisations that were successful in competing in the quality arena.

The US Commerce Department's National Institute of Standards and Technology (NIST) manages the MBNQA programmme in co-operation with the private sector. The American Society for Quality (ASQ) assists NIST with the application review process, preparation of award documents, publicity and information transfer. Any for-profit organisation headquartered in the US or its territories may apply for the MBNQA, including U.S. branches of foreign companies. In 1998, the President and US Congress approved legislation that made education and health care organisations eligible to participate in the award programme.

Awards are presented annually to the following categories: (a) manufacturing; (b) service; (c) small business (500 employees or less); and (d) education and health care. Three awards may be given in each category each year. State and local Baldrige-based award programmes are located in nearly every state and in some communities. These award programmes offer more extensive eligibility opportunities compared to the national Baldrige programme.   Many organisations opt to compete for regional award schemes before considering a Baldrige Award application. Many of the Baldrige Award recipients have also won state quality awards.   In 1998, state and local quality awards programmes received 830 applications.

The MBNQA Criteria for Performance Excellence are designed to help organisations enhance their performance through focus on delivery of ever-improving value to customers, resulting in marketplace success and improvement of overall organisational effectiveness and capabilities.   The Baldrige performance excellence criteria consist of seven categories (see Figure 3.3).   These criteria are used for self-assessment and training and as a tool to develop performance and business processes.   Applicants must submit an application package that consists of three parts: an eligibility determination form, a completed application form and an application report consisting of a business overview and responses to the criteria.

Figure 3.3: MBNQA Criteria for Performance Excellence Framework

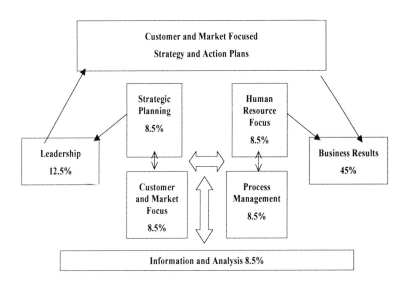

Applications are evaluated by an independent board of examiners composed primarily of private sector experts in quality and business.

Organisations that pass an initial screening are visited by teams of examiners to verify information in the application and to clarify questions that come up during the review. Award applicants receive a feedback report at the conclusion of the review process and interim reports during the award cycle based on the stage of review an application reaches in the evaluation process.

Applicants initially pay a $100 eligibility determination fee. The application fee for manufacturing business and service business categories is $4,500. The application fee for small business, education and healthcare categories is $1,500. Criteria booklets are free if ordered in small numbers from NIST. Booklets in bulk orders may be obtained from ASQ and cost $29.95 each plus shipping and handling costs. Site visit fees are the half the cost for the small business category compared to the cost for the service and manufacturing categories. Site visit fees depend upon the number of examiners assigned and the duration of the visit. In 2000, the site visit fee for not-for-profit educational institutions was $1,200.

Each year, *Quest for Excellence*, the official conference of the MBNQA, provides a forum for award recipients to share their exceptional performance practices with worldwide leaders in business, education, healthcare, and not-for-profit organisations. Traditionally the President of the US presents the awards at a special ceremony in Washington DC. The award programme has the important role of raising awareness about quality by encouraging all US businesses and organisations to set up performance improvement programmes whether or not they intend, or are even eligible, to apply for the award. In 1991, fewer than ten states had award programmes. Now, forty-three states have or are establishing award programmes. Internationally, nearly sixty quality awards are in place.

3.3 Approaches adopted in individual countries

Within these cross-national frameworks, individual countries have often developed their own approaches to quality accreditation. The countries analysed in this review are pioneering in terms of quality service reforms and provide a national perspective on quality accreditation schemes, which can input to the design of the proposed Irish QCS mark (see Chapter Six)[3]. 'One of the most significant trends in the quality field in the last ten years in Europe has been a significant growth in the use of Quality System certification schemes and the business excellence self-assessment mechanisms. During the 1990s, significant effort was invested in developing quality policies on a European level (European Organisations for Quality and Centre for Excellence-Finland, 2000). Similar observations can also be made about systems outside the European Union. National approaches are summarised and compared in Figure 3.4.

3.3.1 Australia

The Australian Quality Council (AQC) is recognised as the main body that assists Australian enterprises in the

Figure 3.4 Accreditation schemes in different countries

	Countries								
Scheme	Irl.	UK.	Dk.	Fin.	Ger.	Australia	Canada	NZ.	USA
EFQM	√	√	√	√*	√				
MBNQA				√		√	√	√	√
ISO Series	Endorsed by the EU and used internationally								
Charter Mark		√							
CAF	EU wide								
Speyer Model					√				

* The present Finnish Quality Award is based on MBNQA but over the 2000-2001 period the National Quality Initiative will encourage greater use of the EFQM Excellence Model.

development and dissemination of knowledge and skills for achieving and sustaining business excellence. 'The AQC is a non-government, not-for-profit, membership-based organisation whose primary role is to support and assist Australian enterprises to achieve world class performance by the adoption of the management principles and practices that are reflected in the Australian Business Excellence Framework, (Australian Quality Council, 2000).'

The Australian Business Excellence Awards are a national variation of the MBNQA. The awards are presented to organisations that have achieved business excellence across all categories in the Australian Business Excellence Framework. The framework has been administered by the Australian Quality Council since 1987. Awards are presented to organisations displaying either a foundation level in business excellence or currently demonstrating best practice. The AQC offers:

• the Award Level to leading Australian organisations currently demonstrating best practice across the Australian Business Excellence Framework

• the Business Improvement Level for organisations using the framework that demonstrate a foundation/progress towards business excellence

• the Award Gold Level which is awarded to previous winners that have sustained their performance levels and continuously improved

- the Australian Business Excellence Prize for organisations which display international best practices throughout the organisation.

The framework incorporates an innovation category, which is a slight variant on the MBNQA criteria and reflects the aim of the framework to assist Australian organisations meet the challenge of globalisation.

3.3.2 Canada

Canada addressed the issue of quality when it launched the Canada Awards for Business Excellence in 1984. This joint industry-government programme developed into the Canada Awards for Excellence in the 1990s, which recognise quality in education, government, healthcare, as well as entrepreneurship, innovation, manufacturing quality and quality service. All sectors of the economy compete on a common set of criteria based on quality principles and practices. The Canadian Quality Criteria for the Public Sector are based on the National Quality Institute (NQI) quality framework. The criteria form the basis of the Canada Awards for Excellence and are also used by state quality organisations as the basis for their quality award programmes (e.g. Quality Council of Alberta awards and the Manitoba Quality Awards). The Canada Awards for Excellence utilise the MBNQA approach and the award ceremony is held yearly as part of Quality Month (October).

The Canadian federal government committed itself to strengthening citizen-centred service delivery by launching the Quality Services Initiative in 1995. Arising from this initiative the Treasury Board of Canada Secretariat, in partnership with the National Quality Institute (NQI), developed *A Framework for Effective Public Service Organisations*. The NQI is a not-for-profit organisation '...committed to enhancing Canada's national well-being through the adoption of quality practices and principles in all sectors'. The framework and supporting documentation are used widely across Canada (National Quality Institute, 1997).

The framework assists departments to achieve 'effective citizen-centred service delivery'. The framework provides the foundations for the Canada Awards for Excellence and is also the basis of quality award programmes run by individual state quality organisations. Self-assessment is carried out on the basis of the NQI Fitness Test and is built around a number of key principles:

- co-operation, teamwork and partnering
- leadership
- primary focus on clients and stakeholder
- respect for the individual and encouragement for people to develop their full potential
- contribution of each and every individual
- process-oriented and prevention-based strategy
- continuous improvements of methods and outcomes
- factual approach to decision making and obligations to stakeholder, including a concern for responsibility to society.

At the level of individual states, the Quality Council of Alberta uses the Canadian Quality Criteria for the Public Sector Framework for its quality awards, which are presented at three levels: commitment, achievement, and excellence. The Manitoba Quality Awards involves external assessment of organisations on the basis of the criteria of the NQI framework. Awards are presented at three levels: bronze for commitment, silver for achievement and gold for excellence. Gold level state award recipients are encouraged to participate in the Canada Awards for Excellence. States present awards for the progress made and organisations then compete at federal level for an annual award.

3.3.3   Denmark
The Danish Public Sector Quality Award was launched in 1997. The award is based on the Business Excellence Model, adapted for a public sector context. All types of public sector institutions, at central and local government levels that have a budgetary and managerial responsibility, and external users may apply for the quality award. The prize is awarded by an award committee that consists of six

members, each having specific knowledge of quality processes and general knowledge of the public sector. The prime minister chairs the committee.

Applicants are awarded points on their achievements according to nine criteria: leadership (100); people management (90); policy and strategy (80); resources (90); processes (140); staff satisfaction (90); customer satisfaction (200); impact on society (60) and business results (150). The maximum sum of points is 1000. Winners of the award can keep it for three years. After this period they have to reapply. The successful award winners are chosen using a seventy-five page self-evaluation manual and site visits by assessor teams

3.3.4 Finland
Since 1994, public administration units have participated in the Finnish Quality Award competition. In 2001 a special public administration class is being introduced and the competition will be based on the European Foundation for Quality Management (EFQM) Excellence Model instead of the present Finnish Quality Award model which is based on Malcolm Baldrige Criteria. To reinforce the transformation the Ministry of Finance launched a two-year project called 'National Quality Initiative 2000-2001' in February 2000. The aim of the initiative was to enhance the use of the EFQM Excellence Model and service charters among public sector organisations. Thirty organisations from all public sector levels participated in the initiative.

3.3.5 New Zealand
The New Zealand Quality Foundation is a trust established by private and public enterprise to improve the overall performance of New Zealand organisations by stimulating and supporting organisational excellence. It presents the following awards for business excellence:
* the National Business Excellence Award – gold level is presented to an organisation displaying a comprehensive approach to excellence with significant results evident across the organisation and this award confirms international recognition of a 'world-class' organisation

- the National Business Excellence Achievement Award – silver level is awarded to an organisation with a comprehensive approach to excellence and with results across most of the organisation

- the National Business Excellence Commendation Award – bronze level is presented to organisations demonstrating a comprehensive approach to excellence with some results in key areas of the organisation

- the National Business Excellence Progress Award – Recognition of progress is given to organisations which have developed and deployed a sound approach to organisational excellence and where results are emerging.

As with Australia and Canada, the New Zealand approach follows closely that adopted by the MBNQA.

3.3.6 United Kingdom

Charter Mark is the UK Government's award scheme for recognising and encouraging excellence in public service. The Charter Mark Awards Scheme has evolved from the Charter Programme set up in 1991 (see Humphreys, 1998). According to government sources, Charter Mark '...provides a good discipline for reviewing a service from the user's perspective, whether as part of a Best Value Review or otherwise. This can lead to more joined-up approaches to service delivery, as this is frequently the direction of change which users want, and can test the assumptions of the organisation against genuine user feedback. (Department of the Environment, Transport and the Regions, 2000)'.

The Service First Unit within the Cabinet Office is responsible for the Charter Mark Awards Scheme, which recognises and encourages excellence in the public service. Charter Mark is based on a voluntary application and applies across the public sector. Any public service body providing a service direct to the public, which manages its own staff and budget, can apply for a Charter Mark. Charter Mark has also been extended to include voluntary organisations providing a service to the public and receiving at least 50 per cent of their income from public sector funds.

Charter Mark was created as a tool to help improve the quality of public services and to help make them more responsive to their customers. To win a Charter Mark, organisations must demonstrate excellence against ten criteria, including high standards of performance, customer satisfaction, complaints handling, and value for money. Since 1999, the scheme criteria have been updated to encourage more partnership working and consultation with front line staff. Charter Mark provides expert independent assessment and detailed feedback on how organisations can improve. Assessors are unpaid and are drawn from varied backgrounds including academics, consultants and retired public servants. There is no limit to the number of winners. Charter Mark focuses on service delivery to the user, and not simply on process.

Since 1999, larger organisations have been encouraged to consider the advantages of submitting applications from individual parts of the organisation where they are clearly autonomous, rather than applying as a whole. An organisation submits the following documents to the Service First Team: an application form, a one-page summary of the main points of the application, a one-page background note about the organisation, ten pages covering the ten criteria and evidence supporting the application.

The written application is marked by two different independent assessors and in most cases the organisation is visited prior to final assessment. Based on the evidence provided by the organisation, detailed feedback is given to the organisation on how to improve their service further and they are informed whether they have won the award. Awards are held for three years, after which organisations must reapply. To win another Charter Mark, organisations must show real improvements in service. Winners receive national and local recognition for providing an excellent service. The winning organisations attend a national awards ceremony where their awards are presented by ministers and they receive a crystal trophy and a certificate signed by the prime minister. They can use the Charter Mark logo on stationery, on vehicles and other equipment for three years. They also obtain expert feedback which over 90 per cent implement.

Many organisations not ready for a full Charter Mark audit, but needing encouragement to improve, undertake self-assessment.

There is currently no application charge, although it is proposed to introduce a £600 fee in 2001. Nationally there are circa 1,200 applications each year, between forty and sixty independent assessors and an annual budget of circa £2 million. The main cost to an organisation is the time spent preparing the application. One local authority with substantial Charter Mark experience estimates that twenty-five to thirty staff days are required in order to prepare an average application. The self-assessment pack costs £25. The self-assessment pack assists in determining the organisation's state of readiness against the ten Charter Mark criteria. Services do not have to complete the self-assessment process before making an application for Charter Mark, but it will help those who do to make basic improvements in readiness for the formal application process.

Enhanced assessors' feedback reports were introduced in 1999 to provide suggestions for improvements for unsuccessful applicants. Many organisations subsequently achieve the Charter Mark standard having implemented these recommendations. Nearly 80 per cent of unsuccessful applicants implement the feedback provided by the assessment team. A special seminar for re-applicants focuses on improvements needed to increase their chance of gaining an award. The introduction of a mentoring system enables unsuccessful applicants to obtain advice on their application and on ways in which they can improve their service from a Charter Mark-holding organisation. Objectivity in assessment is also facilitated by the use of assessors from outside the applicant's region, although there is currently active consideration being given to greater regionalisation of the process.

3.3.7   United States of America (USA)

Since the late 1980s the government in the US has instigated a programme to create 'a Government that works better and costs less.' As part of this programme the

President's Quality Award Program was initiated in 1988 and is administered by the Office of Personnel Management (OPM). The programme is based on Performance Excellence Criteria, which are closely aligned with the Malcolm Baldrige National Quality Award Criteria (MBNQA) (see 3.2.5 above). These criteria have been adapted from the MBNQA criteria to reflect the government environment.

The programme incorporates two awards: the Presidential Award for Quality and the Award for Quality Improvement. The Presidential Award for Quality is applicable to organisations that exhibit 'mature approaches to performance excellence that are well deployed throughout their organisations' (United States Office of Personnel Management (OPM), 2000). The Award for Quality Improvement is relevant to organisations that demonstrate 'early positive approaches to performance excellence that are deployed throughout most of the organisation'.

The programme aims to improve the overall performance and capabilities of federal government organisations. It views customer-driven quality as a core value and a strategic concept for organisations achieving performance excellence. Eligibility for the award programme requires that an organisation must be an autonomous part of the executive branch of federal government (at least one hundred employees) and provide products and services outside of its own organisation or be a support organisation for a cabinet department or an executive agency. The application must cover an entire function, not just a branch or division. An administrative organisation is eligible only for the Award for Quality Improvement.

The President's Quality Award Performance Excellence Criteria are the basis for organisational self-assessment, evaluating an applicant organisation and providing feedback to applicants (United States Offices of Personnel Management (OPM), 2000)

The US President makes the final determination of the organisation(s) to receive the Presidential Award for Quality and OPM makes the final determination of organisations to receive other awards. Awards are presented at the Annual President's Quality Award Program Ceremony held in Washington DC.

Applicants receive a feedback report if it is determined that they will not move to the next step of the award process. That report will contain comments on strengths and opportunities for improvement. Applicants are expected to cover travel costs and 'per diem' costs for site visits.

3.4 Concluding remarks

Over the last decade, quality accreditation schemes have become the norm in most European countries in the public and private sectors. In this chapter, a variety of models has been assessed, reflecting the diversity of quality management models in existence. From this international analysis, it is evident that there is no 'one best approach' to quality. However, in general the models assessed contain the following:

- a self-assessment process prior to formal application to official accreditation
- an application process to an official accreditation scheme involving an application form, external assessment, a site visit, a feedback report and an award or commendation depending upon the assessment
- three levels of awards usually – gold (excellence), silver (achievement) and bronze (commitment) depending upon what stage upon the path to excellence the firm or organisation is at. In some models an additional overall award is presented to the best of the prizewinners
- seven to ten criteria with weightings varying between a customer/people focus or organisational/business focus
- a national recognition to the award winners, to be held for between one and three years in most cases. A review of award winners is normally held annually to ensure standards of excellence are maintained. Award winners are encouraged to participate in annual seminars to disseminate their quality strategies to unsuccessful participants.

The models assessed were based on, or represented, variants of the EFQM Excellence Model or the Malcolm Baldrige Awards in the US. ISO and CAF are 'lighter' frameworks, starter standards or systems, which may be instigated prior to undertaking the more rigorous and detailed accreditation process under MBNQA or the EFQM Excellence Model.

Having established the current context regarding international approaches and practices, we now move to establish the main patterns and characteristics of Irish experiences to date.

CHAPTER 4

Irish Policy Background

4.1 Introduction

In Chapter Two, we defined quality for the purpose of this research as *the extent to which service delivery and/or service outcomes meet with the informed expectations and defined needs of the customer.* In Chapter Two it is also argued that quality accreditation has a central role to play in developing a total quality approach to quality management in the civil and public services. It has been shown in Chapter Three that, internationally, governments are striving to achieve significant improvements in the quality of services provided by their public bodies, often as a core component of wider reform programmes. Quite simply, there has been a growing recognition that QCS is good business, whether in the public or private sectors. That same recognition is also gradually taking root in the Irish public service.

Speaking almost a decade ago, McCumiskey (1992) emphasised the vital importance of quality in public service delivery in Ireland. '[Quality] cannot be divorced from the ongoing changes to standards, values and expectations within the social and political environment. A view which felt that quality was too obtuse for public administration would doom the civil service to a future of perpetual shoddiness in relation to its own particular and immediate areas of activity. In that scenario, the civil service would become particularly unsuitable for the leadership role it is expected to exercise in relation to a myriad of other institutions and undertakings which function in society ... (who) are themselves viewing their world and how they function within it in terms of a continuing search for excellence in a management culture geared to total quality.'

Now, the commitment to significant improvement in the quality of services provided by the Irish public service receives advocacy at the highest level. 'As a government, we recognise clearly that the quality of our public service

directly affects everyone living and working in this country
... the interaction between the customer and the public
service is at the heart of what we are about ... I am asking
ministers and secretaries general to take a lead role in this
process because it requires strong leadership, a change in
organisational culture to put quality service to the customer
first, and it also requires resources (Ahern, 1999).' In fact
there is now a growing recognition that with developing
information and communication technologies (ICTs) the
potential exists, as never before, to transform government
departments and offices into genuinely public service
bodies.

4.2 Strategic Management Initiative (SMI)

The provision of quality services by public bodies to the
wide range of customers they serve is at the heart of the
current programme of public service reform, the Strategic
Management Initiative (SMI). *Delivering Better Government*
(DBG, 1996) perceived '...the achievement of an excellent
service ... for the public as customers as the central thrust
to its report. Indeed, given the significance of the services
delivered by public bodies to the economic and social well-
being of the nation, it can be argued that the Strategic
Management Initiative's ability to deliver significantly
improved services to the citizens that ultimately pay for,
and use, those services will be a litmus test for the success
or otherwise of the SMI as a whole. Equally, failure in this
area could fundamentally undermine external perceptions
of the role and contribution of the public service in modern
Ireland, as well as damage efforts to develop the service as
an 'employer of choice' (see Humphreys and Worth-Butler,
1999)'.

4.3 Building blocks

However, it is important at the outset not to view in
isolation the QCS Initiative which was launched in the civil
service in 1997. Rather it builds upon, and has the
potential to develop further, a number of other major
relevant policy developments at national level. Such
building blocks would include:

- *The Ombudsman Act* (1980)
- *Serving the Country Better* (1985)
- *The Comptroller and Auditor General (Amendment) Act* (1993)
- The Strategic Management Initiative (SMI, launched in 1994)
- *Delivering Better Government* and *Better Local Government* (1996)
- *The Public Service Management Act* (1997)
- *The Freedom of Information Act* (1997)
- The Quality Customer Service Initiative (1997)
- *The Equal Status Act* (2000)[4].

In addition, for many years, a number of individual departments and offices had already made significant, pro-active efforts to improve the quality of services delivered to their customers. Such bodies would include the Department of Agriculture, Food and Rural Development, the Department of Social, Community and Family Affairs and the Office of the Revenue Commissioners (see Humphreys, 1998). As research by Irish Marketing Surveys (1997) showed, these three organisations alone account for over 90 per cent of public contacts with the entire civil service.

4.4 The QCS Initiative (1997)

Drawing upon the work of the original Quality Customer Service Working Group, the QCS Initiative was launched in May 1997 to promote the wider adoption of improved customer service standards by twenty-three departments and offices from November 1997 to October 1999[5]. To facilitate this process, each participating department and office was required to produce a two-year customer action plan. Each plan must indicate how full effect will be given to the following guiding principles and requirements for the delivery of quality customer service.

- *Quality Service Standards*. Publish a statement of standards which outlines the nature and quality of service which customers can legitimately expect and display it prominently at the point of service delivery.

- *Information.* Take a pro-active approach in providing information; it should be clear, timely and accurate, available at all points of contact and meet the needs of people with disabilities. Continue to drive for simplification of rules, regulations, forms, information leaflets and procedures.
- *Timeliness and Courtesy.* Deliver services with courtesy and minimum delay, fostering a climate of mutual respect between the service provider and the customer.
- *Consultation.* Provide a structured approach to meaningful consultation with, and participation by, the customer in relation to the development, delivery and review of services. Involve staff at all levels in the development of service delivery.
- *Choice.* Provide choice, where feasible, in service delivery, including payment methods, location of contact points, opening hours and delivery times. Provide services for those who wish to do business in Irish.
- *Better Co-ordination:* Foster a more co-ordinated and integrated approach to delivery of services.
- *Complaints.* Establish a well publicised, accessible, transparent and simple-to-use system of dealing with complaints about the quality of service provided.
- *Redress.* Introduce a formalised system for customers who are dissatisfied with decisions.
- *Access.* Provide clean, accessible public offices, which ensure privacy, comply with occupational and safety standards and facilitate access for those with disabilities. Give contact names in all telephone and written communications to ensure ease of ongoing transactions.

In June 1997, *Guidelines on Planning for Quality Customer Service* were prepared by the then SMI QCS Working Group and Front-line Group to assist departments and offices in preparing their customer action plans. These Guidelines also incorporated *Public Bodies and the Citizen – The Ombudsman's Guide to Standards of Best Practice for Public Servants*, as well as details of the then Department of Social Welfare's Customer Service Training Course.

When the first customer service action plan period was drawing to a close in 2000, the Taoiseach announced that departments and offices should review and refine their plans to meet the continuing and emergent challenges of the next few years. In this regard, it is also important to note that considerable interest has been shown in the QCS Initiative by the All-Party Oireachtas Committee on the SMI. The committee has already received, or is in the process of considering, presentations from a number of departments and offices: Agriculture, Food and Rural Development; Marine and Natural Resources; Revenue Commissioners; Social, Community and Family Affairs.

4.5 Customer Service Action Plans (1997-2000)

In reviewing and revising their plans for the future, it will be important for departments and offices to draw upon the findings of evaluative research that has already been undertaken during the period of the initial plans. This cross-departmental evaluative work has been undertaken externally and internally.

Through the Committee for Public Management Research (CPMR), two major recent studies in the QCS area have been published (see Humphreys, 1998 and Humphreys et al, 1999). While dealing with wider issues than the 1997 QCS Initiative per se, the first of these studies did include an initial overview of the content and approach adopted by the action plans. Leaving aside the considerable variations in format, style and substance, a number of shortcomings were identifiable at that stage. In particular, there was significant variation between the plans regarding, for example:

- the degree of specification of standards
- how those standards would be delivered
- who should be contacted if further information was required
- the arrangements for complaint and redress
- the clarity and simplicity of language used
- the degree of bi-lingualism (English and Irish)
- steps taken to address the needs of customers with disabilities

- efforts made to spread ownership of the plan internally
- the dissemination arrangements to the public.

For departments and offices with an established QCS track-record, the action plans did not represent a radical departure from more challenging work already in hand. For other bodies however, the QCS concept appeared to be a major new departure deserving encouragement e.g. through the sharing of experiences and best practice.

In addition to external research, the SMI team at the Taoiseach's department has undertaken two evaluative surveys to review progress under the plans at their mid- and end-points.

- The first of these surveys (July 1998) indicated that considerable progress had been made in 'infrastructural' areas such as references to QCS in strategy statements and business plans, the nomination of customer service officers, staff training programmes and improving complaints handling mechanisms. However, far less progress had been made on arrangements for customer surveys and consultation. Indeed, outside the three departments and offices with long-standing commitments to QCS, the conclusion in 1998 was that 'overall progress appears slow'.

- With regard to the results of the second internal survey, undertaken in 1999, a number of key points emerge. While it remained clear that the small number of departments and offices with an established QCS record continued to be well ahead of many others, there was encouraging evidence that more bodies were beginning to engage meaningfully with QCS issues over the period of the plans. In particular, there are indications of concrete efforts being made to improve the information available at points of contact, to improve complaints handling, to engage outside expertise, improve staff training and internal communication. However, despite the advent of the Change Management Fund, available resources are still often referred to by respondents as major constraints on their progress with QCS; and there is certainly evidence in some returns of comparatively limited ownership of the initiative and of low morale.

Overall, available evaluative evidence would suggest that, while there would appear to be some evidence of the widening and deepening of involvement with QCS across the civil service, there is still a considerable distance to travel before customer service values are mainstreamed through the business processes of many departments and offices.

4.6 Challenges to be addressed (2001-2004)

Drawing upon this external and internal evaluative work, a number of significant observations can be made, pointing to further action which needs to be tackled seriously during the next phase of the QCS initiative.

- Too often QCS still appears to be seen as an additional task, rather than as an essential and integral part of departmental business.

- While departments and offices vary in their degree of interface with the general public, few are exempt and quality customer service should not be seen as an issue only for the large operational departments.

- Mainstreaming QCS has very significant implications for the culture and structure of an organisation, which goes well beyond superficial improvements to the handling of enquiries. Acknowledgement of the scale of this challenge within departments can still be quite limited.

- As a result, comparatively few departments and offices appear to have engaged seriously with this challenge to date and, for example, engaged in significant business restructuring to place customer service values centre stage.

- Indeed, excellence in service delivery is best approached as part of an overall drive for quality within the organisation and should not be treated in isolation from other key dimensions, like its investment in its people. Realisation of the crucial people element to achieving QCS is still uneven across the service.

- There also remains a lack of consistency in, and under-utilisation of, quality standards across the service. Subject to continuous review and development, explicit service standards can act as important drivers for change. However, there often appears to remain a marked reluctance to making open commitments to progressive improvements in service standards.

- With a few notable exceptions, there remains a marked reluctance to engage effectively with the public in the development and evaluation of services. Customer surveys and panels are still the exception rather than the rule and, as yet, 'mystery shoppers' have rarely been used. Likewise, little is known about the use made of information obtained from other more simple devices like customer comment cards.

- Similarly, the effective use of the latest developments in information technology (IT) to restructure businesses along customer service lines is still limited. The liberating potential of IT to transform the way we work, rather than simply automate the way we have always worked, must be actively encouraged.

- More work is required to develop and target services to the needs of comparatively disadvantaged groups. In addition, there would appear to be considerable potential for the adoption of accessible language when inter-facing with the public.

- Given the points made above regarding external customers, it is not perhaps surprising that the challenging concepts of QCS have received comparatively little attention to date within organisations. DBG (1996), however, clearly stressed the importance of internal as well as external customers in the improvement of service delivery under SMI.

- Finally, little is known about the extension of the QCS approach in the wider public service. It is certainly evident that, whatever the improvements within organisations in the more integrated delivery of services, major challenges remain before the integration of service delivery to the customer across departments and offices and other agencies becomes a reality. Similarly, there is evidence of considerable innovation at local rather than central government level. Central departments need to be open to bottom-up as well as top-down communication of best practice in QCS (see Humphreys, Fleming and O'Donnell, 1999 CPMR Discussion Paper No.11).

Given the extent, character and significance of the challenges that need to be overcome before the civil service, and wider public service, adopt a quality customer service approach wholeheartedly to their businesses, it was timely and appropriate that a new QCS Working Group was convened in Autumn 1999 (see 1.2 above).

4.7 QCS Working Group (1999 onwards)

Since it was convened in 1999, the QCS Working Group has examined the principles adopted in 1997 and recommended a number of revisions to ensure that the next phase of the QCS Initiative is up to date in the light of subsequent developments.   In particular, three new principles have been enunciated.

- *Equality/Diversity*: Given the advent of the Employment Equality Act (1998) the Equal Status Act (2000), the White Paper on Rural Development and the National Anti-Poverty Strategy (NAPS), there is a need to ensure quality service delivery to the groups covered by the new legislation, as well as those experiencing social exclusion due to socio-economic and/or geographical factors.

- *Official Languages Equality*: In 1997, the provision of services in Irish had been included in the Principle of Choice (see 4.4 above). However, given the proposed Official Languages Equality Bill, the QCSWG felt it appropriate to have a specific and new principle covering the issue of bi-lingualism.

- *Internal Customer*: It was apparent during Phase One of the QCS Initiative that the delivery of quality services to external customers was influenced (in part at least) by the extent to which staff were given the necessary support (e.g. training and resources) by their departments. Back in 1996, DBG had recognised the importance of meeting the needs of the 'internal customer' as an integral part of delivering improved services to the general public.

These three additional principles will guide the development of the next phase of customer action plans, due to be commenced in early 2001. A complete listing of the new guiding principles is provided at Appendix 1. The group feels strongly that these new principles need to be more firmly embedded as core values in organisations. Departments need to ensure that the principles are properly communicated and clearly understood and that they are internalised through increased management support at all levels of business planning, in particular through the partnership process. Those in frontline positions in providing customer services need to feel that they are properly supported throughout the organisation. Meaningful feedback and evaluation mechanisms are also seen by the QCS Working Group as critical to on-going improvement in service delivery.

In taking the QCS Initiative forward, the Working Group has also stressed that best use be made of available and emerging technologies to facilitate improved access to information and improved customer choice through the development of on-line services. Of particular relevance in this regard is the government decision on Information Society (IS) developments and on the adoption of an E-Broker model as the framework within which electronic public services should be delivered. In particular, the group is seeking to promote the next phase of the QCS Initiative in line with the work of the IS Implementation Group, the REACH Initiative and the work of the Connected Government Group within the IS Commission[6]. In relation to the needs of the internal customer in particular, an intranet site is being developed to:

- provide on-line support for the network of departmental QCS officers
- encourage departments and offices to share best practice
- inform people across the service on the latest QCS developments

Guidelines have been issued to inform and ensure consistency of standards for departmental websites.

Standards for departmental websites are to be incorporated into the new round of customer action plans[7]. The group is also keen to see the effective utilisation of IT to help address the current data deficiencies that apply to many of the new grounds for potential discrimination covered by the Equal Status Act 2000. Finally, it must be noted that in addition to the REACH and associated OASIS and BASIS initiatives, on-line services are also currently being provided by the Office of the Revenue Commissioners (ROS), the Land Registry and the FÁS on-line jobs service. An SMI website has been launched as a central information and contact point at http://www.bettergov.ie.

4.8 Programme for Prosperity and Fairness (PPF)

To support these efforts, the need for continued improvement in the quality of public services has been reiterated in the *Programme for Prosperity and Fairness* (PPF). The PPF (2000) stresses that '...improved standards of service follow from a strong focus on the needs of recipients, the setting of challenging standards in service delivery, and making the best use of available resources. In this context, it is essential to provide for consultation with, and feedback from, both the providers and users of the services in order to identify the required improvements and validate the progress being made subsequently in improving service delivery (p.21)'. A strong focus on the needs of customers, effective consultation with the providers and users of services, setting and achieving challenging standards, identifying areas for improvement and monitoring the progress made are all key elements of the QCS improvement process. In fact, PPF (2000) sees it as one of the primary objectives of the modernisation of the public service '...to provide excellent services that meet recipients' needs in a timely and efficient manner (1.4.6)'.

In addition, Annex II of the PPF, which covers public service pay, provides that certain pay increases will be paid in return for the agreement and achievement of specific performance indicators, one of which is '...the implementation of challenging service standards set in consultation with the recipients of the service'[8]. Provision is also made for the establishment of Quality Assurance Groups for each sector, whose remit is to ensure that such performance indicators are sufficiently challenging. Finally, under the PPF, it is envisaged that the principles should apply to all public services and that they should now be extended by each department to include any public service organisation, agency or body for which it has responsibility. In so doing, however, it is acknowledged that many public service bodies have already made significant progress and that developments under PPF in the wider public service will complement work already in hand.

4.9 Developments in the wider public service

While the primary focus of this study is on the civil service, acknowledgement must also be given to the developments to date in the wider public service. In this regard, there is little doubt that individual organisations in the public service have made considerable efforts to significantly improve the quality of service delivered (see Humphreys, Fleming and O'Donnell, 1999). At the sectoral level, it is also evident that significant efforts have been made prior to the advent of the QCS Initiative in 1997. Such examples include:

- the *Code of Practice and Charter of Rights* for the delivery of service to customers of the Revenue Commissioners

- the *Charter of Rights for Hospital Patients* (1992) and *Shaping a Healthier Future* (1994), produced by the Department of Health and Children

- the Department of Agriculture, Food and Rural Development's *Charter of Rights for Farmers*

- the Department of the Environment and Local Government's programme for *Better Local Government* (1996).

In addition, individual public service bodies have taken initiatives. For example:

- An Garda Síochána's *Quality Customer Service Action Plan: Putting People First* (1998)

• the Equality Authority's *Customer Service Action Plan.*

Within the local government sector, *Modernising Government – the Challenge for Local Government* (Department of the Environment and Local Government, 2000) recognises that delivering quality customer services is at the heart of the current reform programme. Accordingly, it launches a range of common *Service Indicators* for each local authority, which will help individual authorities benchmark their performance against others. Progress against these indicators is to be reported in the 2000 series of annual reports, with the intention of rolling out this quantitative approach to service and standards setting.

4.10 Involvement with existing quality accreditation schemes

Two main quality accreditation schemes operate at present in Ireland(see Chapter Three). These are ISO 9000 and the Q-Mark.

4.10.1 ISO 9000

'ISO is the international standard for quality systems which provides a basis for assessing your organisation, or part thereof, against objective requirements of organisational discipline and control, traceability and the like (Bendell, Boulter and Kelly, 1994).' Under ISO 9000, an organisation implements a quality system and applies to the National Standards Authority of Ireland (NSAI) for accreditation by submitting an application form and questionnaire accompanied by the quality manual and the application fee. The organisation's quality manual is assessed by an appointed assessor and deemed to be satisfactory or returned for amendments. An agreed on-site assessment is conducted by the NSAI audit team and the findings are contained in a detailed report sent to the organisation. The organisation may have to conduct corrective action or may be recommended for registration. Organisations recommended for registration will be subjected to the NSAI Review and Approval Process. Once registration is granted, the organisation will be subject to on-going surveillance inspections. Certain public sector organisations may require suppliers to hold a Q-Mark.

The initial application costs from £250 to £580 (plus VAT) depending on the number of employees in the organisation. Assessment and surveillance costs are charged twice yearly at £446 per auditor, per day (plus VAT). The annual registration fee varies from £200 to £500 depending on the number of employees. Detailed information on standards is available from NSAI for between £15 and £25 per publication.

ISO 9000 is used widely by the private sector, including financial institutions, IT software and hardware companies, the professions (including architects, engineers and lawyers), healthcare organisations and the transport sector (see NSAI, 1999). There has also been involvement by some commercial semi-state companies, including Aer Lingus, Aer Rianta, Bord Gais and the ESB. However, it is also important to note that non-commercial, public service organisations have been involved, including some health boards, local authorities, as well as the Office of Public Works, sections of FÁS and the Motor Tax Office (Wexford).

4.10.2 The Q-Mark

The Q-Mark is promoted by Excellence Ireland as an accreditation framework to encourage benchmarking, aimed at optimising the competitiveness of Irish business. The Q-Mark is based on the principles of the Business Excellence Model (BEM). The model that Excellence Ireland applies is derived from the EFQM Excellence Model. It aims to provide a broader ambit of quality service than ISO 9000. The Q-Mark is a diagnostic framework that links together all existing quality improvement schemes within an organisation.

The formal process for application and assessment commences with the organisation completing a first-time submission document. It requires evidence of what the organisation is doing and the results being achieved under each element of the Q-Mark model. Assessment is carried out by an Excellence Ireland assessor based on the submission document and a scheduled on-site visit. A detailed assessment report is prepared by the assessor, outlining strengths, areas for improvement, and giving a score for each element of the model. The report then goes to the Independent Approvals Board which meets every quarter, for judgement.

Organisations achieving the 50 per cent (of a total of 400 points) pass mark for accreditation receive a certificate in recognition of their achievement. Holders of the Q-Mark are audited annually by registered auditors to ensure that the required standards are maintained. An independent feedback report assists the organisation's business improvement agenda. It can lead to national and public recognition through the display of the Q-Mark logo on stationery and participation at prestigious awards events. The Q-Mark provides access to the National Awards Programme and listing in both the Excellence Ireland Directory of Quality Organisations and website.

Excellence Ireland present awards at three levels (a Foundation Mark, Q-Mark, and the Mark Excellence) under the 'Business Excellence Recognition Marks' system. Annual national award ceremonies are held to recognise the best performing organisations within the scheme. The Q-Mark was originally based on ISO 9000 but more recently has transferred to the EFQM model. Within the public sector, a number of organisations have been involved including Bord na Móna, the ESB, FÁS and the Food Safety Authority.

4.11 Concluding remarks

To date, and in contrast to other countries, engagement with either national or cross-national quality accreditation schemes in Ireland has been comparatively limited. In the absence of wide-spread engagement with well-established schemes such as ISO 9000 and the EFQM, the emphasis has often been on initiatives within individual organisations seeking to raise their quality of service provision, as part of their commitment to best practice. In exploring constructive ways to take the next phase of the QCS Initiative forward, a new recognition scheme for the public service could have a very significant contribution to make.

To further internalise the new principles and to raise both awareness and morale, a Quality Customer Service (QCS) Mark could be introduced across the public service. This would allow achievement to be acknowledged and provide a platform to facilitate the sharing of best practice among organisations.

There is therefore little doubt that with the gradual progress of the SMI and, in particular, the promotion and extension of the QCS Initiative from 1997 onwards in the civil and wider public service, awareness of quality management issues and approaches is growing. In this context, the time is opportune for the wider adoption of appropriate accreditation arrangements as an incentive to progressive change.

CHAPTER 5

Developing A Quality Accreditation Framework

5.1 Introduction

Building upon the preceding analyses of concepts and of international and national arrangements, the purpose of this chapter is to evaluate the different approaches to quality customer service, in order to develop an accreditation framework appropriate to the Irish public service at its present stage of QCS development. These preceding analyses of international and national arrangements suggest that accreditation systems broadly operate on two levels.

- There are over-arching frameworks aimed at providing a comprehensive diagnosis for the organisation as a whole, e.g. the EFQM, CAF and Canadian approaches. The emphasis is on a balanced approach to organisational effectiveness or fitness for purpose, with a focus on the customer as one of several aspects of overall performance. Such approaches can be defined as high-level accreditation frameworks.

- In addition, supporting systems can be identified that can either be used alone to focus on specific aspects of performance, such as quality customer service, or to complement the high-level frameworks, e.g. the ISO 9000 series, the UK Charter Mark and Investors in People (IIP) (see 5.3.1 below).

5.2 High-level accreditation frameworks

All high-level accreditation systems focus on results and on the factors that influence results (see figure 5.1). Looking across the high-level frameworks, we see a focus on seven key themes, leadership, strategy and planning, people, organisational management, processes, the customer and civil responsibility (the latter in the EFQM, MBNQA and CAF frameworks). Because of their significance for later

Figure 5.1: Themes across high-level frameworks

	Excellence Model	Canadian Framework	Baldrige Framework	Common Assessment Framework
Leadership	Leadership	Leadership	Leadership	Leadership
Strategy and planning	Strategy and planning	Planning	Strategic planning	Policy and strategy
People	• People management • People satisfaction	• People focus	• Human resource focus	• Human resource management • People results
Organisational management	• Resources • Business results	• Organisational performance • Supplier/ partnering focus	• Information and analysis • Business results	• External partnerships and resources • Key performance results
Processes	Quality systems and processes	Process management	Process management	Process and change management
Customer	Customer satisfaction	Citizen/client focus	Customer focus	Customer/citizen-orientated results
Civic responsibilities	Impact on society		Organisational responsibility and citizenship	Impact on society

discussion, each of these key themes deserves further elaboration here.

5.2.1 Leadership
Overall, three approaches to leadership can be identified within these frameworks:

(a) Providing strategic direction
Leaders have key roles to play in developing and disseminating the mission, vision and values of the organisation, as well as relating them to objectives, key success factors, priorities and accountability. Leadership also involves retrospective review and seeking future opportunities for the organisation.

(b) Achieving change
This involves recognising, motivating and empowering people, as well as supporting learning. Leaders are role models for a culture of excellence, fostering values for long-term success. Reward and recognition for senior managers are linked to quality principles. Achieving change also

includes the development of management systems to ensure: responsibility and accountability; the sharing of leadership; continuous improvement; teamwork and open communication.

(c) Focusing efforts on customer service
Leadership involves both creating and balancing value for customers and stakeholders, as well as active involvement by leaders with customers, partners and representatives of society.

In addition, two further leadership themes are included in the North American frameworks:

(d) Performance review (MBNQA)
Leaders are involved in assessing the 'health' of their organisations and translating findings into priorities for improvement, as well as opportunities for innovation and reinvention. It involves dissemination of priorities to everyone, including suppliers and key customers, using the findings to increase leadership effectiveness and for effective management.

(e) Citizenship and responsibility to society (MBNQA and Canada)
This includes: considering responsibility to society in decision-making processes; assessing the impact of products or services; anticipating public concerns; ensuring ethical business practices; sharing ideas or practices on quality improvement internally and externally; and supporting communities.

5.2.2 Strategy and planning
Planning features strongly as a theme in all four frameworks. The focus is on developing strategies and policies, implementing those strategies and policies, and measuring achievement.

(a) Developing strategies and policies
A clear stakeholder-focused strategy is required in both the CAF and EFQM frameworks, so that organisational policy and strategies are based on information relating to present and future needs of stakeholders. In the MBNQA model, the strategy development process includes gathering and

analysing information on: customers and the market; supplier/partner capabilities and needs; and organisational, human resource and operational competitiveness and capabilities. In the Canadian model, key improvement issues are identified by drawing on information from clients, suppliers, partners and employers.

(b) Implementing strategies and policies
The Canadian model requires an improvement plan to be developed which is communicated both internally and externally and is regularly reviewed and monitored. The EFQM and CAF require policies and strategies to be implemented through a process of cascading, aligning, prioritising, agreeing and communicating plans, objectives and targets. The MBNQA framework requires the development/deployment of an action plan which documents the key human resources required, resources to be allocated, key performance measures to track progress and how the plan is to be communicated and deployed. In addition, performance projections and benchmarking are required.

(c) Measuring achievement
All four frameworks require progress against strategic objectives to be monitored and reviewed. The MBNQA framework explicitly requires that monitoring and review should be based on gathering and analysing relevant data and information. The Canadian model requires formal assessment using criteria reflecting quality principles. The EFQM and CAF require policies, strategies, processes and plans themselves to be constantly monitored for their appropriateness.

5.2.3   People
A very strong focus on people is a common feature of all four high-level frameworks. This focus relates to how human resources are planned, managed and developed in order to enable each individual to reach her/his full potential within the organisation. It recognises human resources as the prime resource of any organisation and the need for staff to be enabled to contribute effectively to

achieving the organisation's goals.   The frameworks also emphasise the importance of people feeling valued and respected, being empowered and included in improvements. Overall, five key features can be identified: planning; managing HR systems and processes; developing skills and competencies; empowering and communicating; reward and recognition; employee well being and satisfaction.

(a) Planning people resources
The need for planning is identified in all frameworks.   More explicitly, the CAF stresses the need to plan, manage and improve human resource policies and to align the plan with the organisational policy, strategy, structure and processes. The Canadian framework identifies the need for human resource planning to support the organisation's goals and objectives.

(b) Managing HR systems and processes
All frameworks identify the need to have appropriate HR systems and processes in place for recruitment, selection and performance management.   CAF stresses that recruitment and career development are managed in relation to fairness of employment and equality of opportunity.   The MBNQA framework includes requirements that: (i) recruitment takes into account key performance requirements, the diversity of local communities and fair work practices; (ii) performance management systems support high performance; and (iii) work systems are designed, organised and managed to promote co-operation/collaboration, individual initiative, innovation, flexibility, as well as keeping up to date with changing business needs.

(c) Developing skills and competencies
The need to pin point, develop and sustain skills and competencies is identified in the EFQM and CAF frameworks.   The MBNQA model recognises the need to identify characteristics and skills required by potential employees.   In terms of providing education, training and development, it is suggested that a balance is required between short-term and long-term organisation/employee needs, and that input should be sought from employees and

managers on training and education needs. The emphasis in the Canadian model is on continuous learning, encouraging people to expand individual skills and identifying training and development required to ensure that the organisation achieves its goals. It also requires the effectiveness of all training to be evaluated.

(d) Empowering people and improving communication
The EFQM and CAF frameworks include empowering people and improving communication as key features. The focus in the MBNQA model is on ensuring effective communication, co-operation and knowledge/skill sharing across units, functions and locations as appropriate. The Canadian framework emphasises the need for a participatory environment and ensuring everyone understands the strategic direction and that all are committed to achieving goals and purpose. In addition, it requires the involvement of people in improvement initiatives, encouraging and implementing people's suggestions and ideas, and encouraging people to innovate and take risks to achieve goals.

(e) Reward and recognition
In the MBNQA, EFQM and CAF frameworks, the emphasis is on how recognition and related reward practices can reinforce high performance and how people are rewarded, recognised and cared for. The Canadian model suggests that recognition systems should focus on the contribution of people, linking recognition to the quality principles and quality improvement objectives of the organisation.

(f) Ensuring employee well-being and satisfaction
The North American frameworks include explicit criteria for ensuring employee well being, with a focus on the workplace environment; health and safety; involving employees in identifying and addressing issues; employee support (MBNQA); and identifying and removing barriers that prevent people doing their best work (Canadian). Results in relation to employee satisfaction and well being are also characteristic of the EFQM and CAF frameworks. These results relate to people perceptions, management and working conditions, employee participation, motivation and morale.

5.2.4 Organisational management

Organisational management themes relate to how external relationships and internal resources are planned and managed to support the organisation's policy and strategic direction, and the effective operation of its processes. The North American models have a stronger emphasis on suppliers and partnering. In the MBNQA model, criteria relate to the selection of products and services from suppliers or partners, incorporating performance requirements into supplier processes, ensuring that they are met, controlling costs, and providing incentives for suppliers to contribute to the organisation's performance.

In the Canadian approach, criteria relate to selecting capable suppliers and service providers using appropriate information and criteria; establishing co-operative working relationships with key suppliers and service providers; and encouraging innovation to assure and improve the quality of services and products. Also included is sharing information with suppliers and service providers to enable them to improve services and to involve them in the development of new products or services. The emphasis in the development of partnerships in the CAF and EFQM is aimed mainly towards benchmarking and sharing information on performance.

5.2.5 Processes

All four frameworks feature processes as a key theme, e.g. 'value-adding transformations involving people and other resources' (National Quality Institute, 1997). The Treasury Board also states that

> It is important to focus on the key processes and to simplify and prioritise them as they relate to the primary mission of the organisation. It is these key processes that need to be continually analysed and improved. Key processes in public service organisations relate to those services and support processes that are essential to running the organisation. Vital to identifying, evaluating and improving key processes is linking them to strategic intent.

Overall, this theme relates to the design, management and improvement of processes to support the organisation's strategy, so that it can meet the needs of customers and stakeholders and generate added value for them. There is a need to identify, from the goals in the implementation plans, priorities for improving the processes; there is also a need to ensure that design, product and service delivery, support processes, and supplier and partnering processes are customer-focused.

There is considerable difference between frameworks in terms of how this theme is dealt with. The least prescriptive approach is that found in the EFQM model where the requirements are that processes are systematically designed, managed and improved, as needed, using innovation in order to fully satisfy and generate increasing value for customers and other stakeholders. Products and services are designed and developed based on customer needs and expectations. Customer relationships are managed and enhanced. In contrast, the Canadian approach places considerable emphasis on defining and documenting key processes capable of delivering customer needs; on process control and improvement; and on the effectiveness of the design process for new services and continuous improvement.

5.2.6 Customer

As previously indicated, all four frameworks seek to integrate customer service and quality principles as central themes into the leadership, strategy and planning, and process aspects of each framework. However, there are some differences between the European and North American frameworks in how the concept of the customer is addressed, e.g. both North American frameworks have separate categories for 'Customer Focus' and 'Citizen and Client Focus'. Because of their comparative unfamiliarity, these foci merit specific consideration.

(a) MBNQA approach to customer focus

Broadly speaking this approach has three main aspects:

- *customer and market knowledge* – determining target customers, listening and learning to determine key requirements and drivers of purchase decisions (including former and potential customers), using that information (including complaints) in marketing, product planning and business developments on a continuous basis

- *customer relationships* – determining key access mechanisms, key customer contact requirements and sensitising all employees in the response chain to them; complaint management by analysing complaints for use in organisational improvement, building relationships with customers for repeat business and positive referrall; and keeping approaches current with business needs

- *customer satisfaction determination* – processes, measurement methods and data to determine customer satisfaction; customer follow-up for prompt and actionable feedback; obtaining and using information relative to competitors/benchmarks; and keeping approaches current with business needs.

(b) Canadian Approach to citizen and client focus
This approach includes:

- *hearing the voice of the client or stakeholder* – defining clients, stakeholders and client groups; gathering, analysing and evaluating information to determine needs; gathering and using information on the future needs of current or potential clients

- *managing client and stakeholder relationships* – achieving organisational consensus on the importance of meeting documented service standards and achieving client or stakeholder satisfaction; having methods and processes in place that make it easy for clients or stakeholders to provide input, seek assistance and complain; responding promptly and effectively to inquiries and complaints; developing a good level of client or stakeholder confidence in services or products through meeting service delivery standards or product specifications

- *measuring client and stakeholder satisfaction* – to gain information for improvement
- *positive Results* – having good levels and trends of performance in dealing with inquiries, complaints and appeals.
- *continuous improvement* – through evaluation and using the findings to improve citizen or client focus.

5.2.7   Civic responsibilities

Finally, the high-level frameworks also focus on how organisations accept social responsibility and consider the impact of what they do on society. As noted previously, the MBNQA framework includes in its *leadership* section criteria for 'organisation responsibility and leadership'. This includes:

- *responsibilities to the public* – how an organisation addresses the impacts on society of its products, services and operations, how it anticipates public concerns with current and future products, services and operations, and how it ensures ethical business practices in all stakeholder transactions and interactions
- *support of key communities* – how the organisation, leaders and employees, actively support and strengthen its key communities.

The CAF has a specific category for impact on society, focusing on the manner in which the organisation achieves and satisfies the needs and expectations of the local, national and international communities. Assessment is based on results relating to improved perception by society of the organisation's performance, the prevention of harm and nuisance in the preservation and sustainability of resources, and other indicators of societal responsibility. The EFQM Model has a specific category for society results, which is based on perception measures and performance indicators.

5.2.8   Overview of high-level frameworks

For ease of reference, the key quality concepts underpinning the high-level frameworks analysed in this research are summarised in Figure 5.2.

Figure 5.2 Concepts of quality in higher level frameworks

Leadership	• Providing strategic direction • Achieving change • Focusing efforts on customer service • Performance review • Citizenship and responsibility to society
Strategy and planning	• Developing strategies and policies - stakeholder-focus - derived from overall strategic direction • Implementing strategies and policies • Measuring achievement
People	• Planning people processes • Managing HR systems and processes • Developing skills and competencies • Empowering people and improving communication • Reward and recognition • Employee well being and satisfaction
Organisational management	• External relationships, suppliers and partnering • Internal resources • Information management and analysis
Processes	• Design, management and improvement of processes • Customer focus of processes and increasing value for customers • Reform processes and change management • Project management and resource allocation
Customer	• Customer and client focus • Customer and market knowledge • Customer satisfaction and relationships
Civic responsibilities	• Responsibilities to the public/society • Support of key communities and society results • Impact on society

Sources: *Excellence Model, Baldridge Model, CAF and Canadian Framework for Effective Public Service Organisations*

5.3 Supportive frameworks

As noted earlier, in a number of public administrations supportive frameworks have also been developed. These frameworks can contribute in their own right to improving quality services and can also support the involvement of organisations in the high-level frameworks (see Figure 5.3). While both the ISO 9000 series and the Charter Mark have already been discussed in detail in Chapter Three, the UK Investors in People Programme has not previously been discussed and the key features of this programme are now summarised.

Figure 5.3: The relationship between high-level and supporting accreditation frameworks

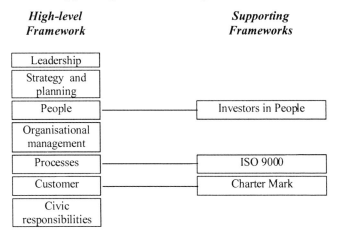

5.3.1 Investors in People

The *Investors in People National Standard* is used extensively in UK private and public sector organisations to relate employee development to organisational goals and performance. In this way the Investors in People framework can support the 'people' element of high-level frameworks. Investors in People is based on four key principles:

- a commitment from the top to develop all employees
- a regular review of the training and development needs of employees and a plan to meet those needs

- action to train and develop individuals throughout their employment
- measurement of the outcome of the organisation's investment in training and development.

From these four principles twelve standards form the basis of the accreditation framework, which is detailed in Appendix 2.

5.4 Towards a framework for accreditation in the Irish public services

Based on the findings outlined so far, the first issue to be explored in developing proposals for an accreditation framework for the Irish public services is the level at which a quality customer service (QCS) mark framework should be pitched. Is it the high-level framework that is required, and is this feasible? Alternatively, would a more appropriate approach be to start small, by focusing at first on the customer element? This could then be developed further on an incremental basis into a high-level framework, such as the EFQM.

QCS relates specifically both to the customer and to the process elements of high-level frameworks, as well as supporting systems such as Charter Mark and ISO 9000. However, these customer and process elements are inextricably linked with the other elements of organisational performance. Individual elements of performance, and of course organisational performance as a whole, impact significantly on the quality and effectiveness of services, and on customer perceptions of the organisation. That is the context in which any attempt to decide in favour of either a high-level framework or a lighter customer-focused one for the Irish public service must be approached. That decision must also take account of the fact that engagement to date by the Irish public service in high-level frameworks has been comparatively limited (see Chapter 4); and further, many public service bodies are commencing from a comparatively low stage of development in QCS terms.

Within the terms of reference of this study, an accreditation framework could be developed that would focus specifically on QCS, based around the concepts found in the customer and process elements of the high-level frameworks and those included in Charter Mark and ISO 9000. Account could also be taken of aspects of organisational performance such as leadership and people management that are required to underpin quality customer service. Such an approach would be similar to that found in the four high-level frameworks.

This is the model for a framework for QCS accreditation in the Irish civil service which we propose. An outline of such an approach is given at Figure 5.4.

Figure 5.4: The emerging framework for QCS accreditation

5.4.1   Building a customer focus

The preceding analysis suggests that a central feature in developing quality customer services is achieving a customer focus to service delivery. Key elements of building a customer focus seen in other frameworks include:

- designing and developing customer services based on customer needs and expectations. This may include steps such as identifying target customers and determining their key requirements, increasing public access to services, or making explicit the need for polite and helpful service

- actively seeking the views of customers and empowering them. Steps may include increasing openness and understanding, improving access to and the quality of information provided, citizen charters and complaints procedures. Providing information to customers about the service that they should expect and the choices available to them, and using feedback to improve services, are key features of the Charter Mark framework

- managing customer relationships, by building a consensus throughout the organisation of the importance of meeting documented service standards and achieving customer satisfaction, by determining key access mechanisms and customer contact requirements, by reacting promptly to customer feedback and building relationships with customers for repeat business and positive referral
- evaluation and continuous improvement to customer service using customer results and feedback are key features of Charter Mark and high-level frameworks, particularly the Canadian model.

As indicated in Chapter Four, the twelve new principles developed to guide the next phase of the QCS Initiative, while not all-embracing, do provide a basis upon which to develop a more comprehensive framework. As previously suggested, building a customer focus would also need to be supported by customer-focused themes running through other aspects of organisational performance such as leadership, strategy and planning and the management and development of people. Approaches seen in the four high-level frameworks would suggest that a number of principles need to support the quality customer service accreditation.

- Leaders should be centrally involved in building a customer focus within the organisation, and developing external customer relationships and public perceptions.
- Building a customer focus, designing services to meet customer needs and expectations, and improving customer service need to be seen as a strategic priority and a central theme in policy and planning.
- Building a customer focus and improving service delivery need to be central themes in people management and employee development.

5.4.2 Processes

As indicated in the description of high-level frameworks, processes also need to be designed and improved to fully satisfy customers and stakeholders and to generate increasing value for customers. In the Canadian model, the focus is on the key processes in the delivery of services and on documenting those processes, monitoring them for consistency and analysing problems, identifying root causes and taking corrective action. Continuous improvement of processes involving clients and suppliers, and benchmarking to identify opportunities for improvement, are also key features in the Canadian model. Processes also need to be managed to ensure customer orientation and involvement. As suggested in the CAF, this could include ensuring processes increase openness and understanding between customers and the organisation, increase public access to services, and empower customers/citizens.

5.4.3   Customer results

As suggested in the comparative review of the high-level frameworks, customer results could refer to what the organisation has achieved in its efforts to meet the needs and expectations of customers, stakeholders, clients and citizens. Three possible aspects could be:

- customer satisfaction – measures/current levels and trends, and indicators of customer satisfaction
- the results of actions taken to improve customer satisfaction
- the results of actions taken to empower customers.

5.5 The way forward

The purpose of this chapter has been to review the range of concepts of quality that are used in high-level and supporting frameworks used in quality accreditation schemes, both nationally and internationally, in terms of their possible usefulness for quality customer accreditation in the Irish civil and public service. Ideally, such quality accreditation could take the form of a high-level framework aimed at continuous improvement of organisational performance overall, and as a result improve quality customer service.

A more pragmatic and feasible alternative would be to develop a set of accreditation criteria that would focus specifically on the customer aspects of service and meeting customer needs, but also including some of the themes contained in high-level frameworks, such as leadership, planning and strategy and investment in people. Such a medium-level framework could then be developed further over time towards a high-level framework. The essential difference between the two approaches would be whether a 'big-bang' or incremental approach would be more appropriate. Approaches to reform in recent times in Ireland have been based on the incremental and consensus-building approach, which is widely believed to be less disruptive and more likely to succeed in the longer term.

CHAPTER 6

A QCS Mark for the Irish Public Service

6.1 Introduction

By critically evaluating current arrangements in Ireland, and drawing upon best practice here and elsewhere, this research seeks to provide some objective and practical guidance on how a QCS Mark scheme for the Irish public service could best be introduced. Before exploring such a scheme in more detail, it is worth recapping the main reasons why a QCS Mark for the Irish public service could make a beneficial contribution to taking the next phase of the QCS initiative forward.

Drawing upon the experience of other countries, and the feedback received during the course of this project from those actively involved in the promotion of QCS at central, departmental and institutional levels, a number of reasons can be identified:

- While considerable progress has been made by individual public bodies, and though there has been considerable encouragement provided by the QCS Initiative from 1997 onwards, feedback from departments and offices still suggests that progress has been far from even across the service and that there is a continuing need to (re)invigorate the change process. In this context, the development and promotion of an effective service-wide system of accreditation and recognition (i.e. a QCS Mark) could have a key role to play in the next phase of the QCS Initiative.

- In particular, a well-designed QCS Mark Scheme could assist the internal and external promotion of a quality customer service, by raising awareness and morale, and acting as a driver for progressive change. Properly designed and managed, it could promote healthy competition within and between organisations. There is little doubt that throughout the service, there are champions of quality customer service but there is an absence of recognition for the difficult and challenging work that is being done. A QCS Mark scheme would allow such achievement to be acknowledged and replicated more widely.

- Such a development could also have major implications for the promotion of a benchmarking approach to QCS by the public service and provide an invaluable platform to facilitate the sharing of best practice between public service organisations. By generating comparable information across the public service, it will allow organisations to compare their performance with others.

Given the current early stage of development of many public service bodies in their adoption of quality management approaches to the delivery of services, it is also clear from the feedback received during this research programme that such a QCS Mark scheme should be simple but meaningful, challenging but attainable. Its administration would have to be robustly objective and fair. While representing a prestigious achievement within itself, a new QCS Mark for the Irish public service could also provide an opportunity for organisations to progress towards a higher level internationally recognised framework such as EFQM.

6.2 Some key management challenges

Quality accreditation has a central role to play in developing a total quality approach to quality management in the civil and public services. From the analysis of available research evidence in Chapter Two, a working definition of quality for the purpose of this research was cited as *the extent to which service delivery and/or service outcomes meet with the informed expectations and defined needs of the customer.* Achievement of quality therefore requires a number of significant challenges to be addressed. These challenges include:

- The promotion and acceptance of quality customer service needs to be seen as one of the key principles of public service delivery. To achieve this, quality needs to be an integral part of services and to be seen as the responsibility of everyone involved in the design and delivery of services.

- Visible and effective leadership at the most senior level is a pre-requisite for building a customer focus in public service bodies, together with the championing of quality customer service values throughout the organisation and its business processes.

- Quality public services need to be developed, designed and delivered in a manner which is genuinely customer-focused and responsive to changing customer needs and expectations.

- Within the public service in particular, the complex relationship between the customer and the range of other stakeholders (including the staff, the taxpayer and elected representatives) needs to be understood and managed effectively to minimise conflicts of interests in terms of what is understood as quality customer service.

- Challenges relate also to the nature of public services, their diversity and complexity, and to the fact that roles, responsibilities, functions and budgets are externally imposed upon public service organisations. Nonetheless, responsibility for the design and delivery of quality services rests primarily with the organisation.

- Quality customer service relates to how services are perceived by customers and how these experiences relate to expectations. Quality customer services need to be refocused on the customer and this will require citizen participation in the design and delivery of services. Real participation will require customer and citizen involvement to move beyond consultation towards the promotion of partnership and negotiation between all stakeholders.

It is also abundantly clear from the literature that addressing these challenges effectively raises issues that strike at the heart of an organisation's mission and purpose.

6.3 International experiences

The research findings reported in Chapter Three indicate

that the majority of OECD countries have been seeking to implement quality policies within their public services since the mid to late 1980s. These approaches range from engagement with internationally recognised, multi-faceted high-level accreditation frameworks or support arrangements, such as the European Foundation for Quality Management Excellence Model (EFQM), the Speyer Quality Award, the Malcolm Baldrige National Quality Award and the ISO 9000, to specific initiatives such as the UK Charter Mark focused explicitly on improving customer service. Experiences in a range of individual countries have also been reviewed in some detail: Australia, New Zealand, Denmark, Finland, Canada, the US and the UK.

At one level, this international comparison of public service quality accreditation systems highlights the simple fact that there is no one 'best way' in quality accreditation, but instead a range of approaches which can be tailored to meet individual national circumstances. Even so, comparative cross-national analysis of accreditation schemes does allow the identification of common themes which are equally relevant to the Irish situation. International experience indicates that most schemes have:

- an initial self-assessment process prior to formal application for official accreditation

- an application process to an official accreditation scheme which involves an application form, external assessment, a site visit, a feedback report and an award or commendation depending upon the assessment

- three levels of awards – gold (excellence), silver (achievement) and bronze (commitment) depending upon what stage upon the path to excellence the firm or organisation is at; in some models, an additional overall award is presented to the best of the prize-winners; such an award is normally presented at a high-profile event

- national recognition for the award winners with an award normally held for between one and three years; a review of award winners is normally held annually to ensure standards of excellence are maintained; award

winners are encouraged to participate in annual
seminars to disseminate their quality strategies to
unsuccessful participants
- most assessments are based on a range of criteria with
  weightings varying between a customer/people focus or
  organisational/business focus.

6.4 Potential evaluation criteria

Following their formal endorsement by government decision
in July 2000, and given the context of the current stage of
development of the QCS Initiative in Ireland (see Chapter
Four), it would make sense to put the twelve new Guiding
Principles for Customer Service Action Plans (2001-2004) at
the core of the evaluative framework for a new QCS Mark in
Ireland. Many of these principles have already been tested
in the first round of the QCS Initiative and the revised
principles are the result of careful deliberation by the QCS
Working Group which is tasked with taking the next phase
of the QCS Initiative forward, including its roll-out to the
wider public service.

In summary, the revised principles are:

1. Ensure staff are recognised as internal customers and
   are properly supported and consulted with regard to
   service delivery issues.

2. Take a pro-active approach to providing clear, timely
   and accurate information that is available at all points
   of contact and meets the requirements of people with
   specific needs. Continue to simplify rules, regulations,
   forms, information leaflets and procedures.

3. Publish and display QCS standards that outline the
   nature and quality of service that external customers
   can expect.

4. Deliver quality services with courtesy, sensitivity and
   the minimum delay, in a climate of mutual respect
   between provider and customer.

5. Provide clean and accessible public offices, which ensure
   privacy, comply with occupational and safety standards
   and facilitate access for people with specific needs.

6. Where feasible, provide choice in service delivery in terms of payment methods, location of contact points, opening hours and delivery times. Use available and emerging technologies to ensure maximum access and choice, and quality of delivery.

7. Ensure the rights to equal treatment established by equality legislation, and accommodate diversity, so as to contribute to equality for the groups covered by that legislation. Identify and work to eliminate barriers to access to services for people experiencing poverty and social exclusion, as well as those facing geographic barriers to services.

8. Provide quality services through Irish and/or bilingually and inform customers of their rights to choose to be dealt with through one or other of the official languages.

9. Provide a structured approach to meaningful consultation with, and participation by, the customer in relation to the development, delivery and review of services. Ensure meaningful evaluation of service delivery.

10. Foster a more co-ordinated and integrated approach to delivery of public services.

11. Maintain a well-publicised, accessible, transparent and simple-to-use system of dealing with complaints about the quality of service provided.

12. Similarly, maintain a formalised, well-publicised, accessible, transparent and simple-to-use system of appeal or review for customers who are dissatisfied with decisions in relation to services.

Full details of the new Guiding Principles are given in Appendix 1.

However, it is also important to stress that, while the achievement of demonstrable progress on operationalising these principles could form the core of a new QCS Mark Scheme, it is also clear from the analysis of leading accreditation schemes in other countries, as well as cross-nationally, that all the key elements for an accreditation scheme would not be addressed in this way. In particular, international best practice (see Figure 5.2) suggests a number of additional key factors that would merit inclusion in a new scheme:

- strong and demonstrable commitment to QCS throughout an organisation as well as affirmative leadership at its most senior levels
- effective strategic planning to ensure the mainstreaming of QCS throughout the business
- significant investment in the people required to develop and deliver quality services.

A core feature of this research has been a detailed analysis of the range of accreditation frameworks in use internationally. Based upon these findings, together with a review of the current position in Ireland, an appropriate framework for the introduction of a QCS mark for the Irish public service is outlined below. While the Committee for Public Management Research (CPMR) would not normally include such detailed proposals in its research reports, the draft scheme outlined below is being put forward to help inform discussion and debate at the appropriate levels.

6.5   A QCS Mark for the Irish public service: an outline scheme

There is a compelling case for introducing an award scheme for recognising excellence in quality customer service in the Irish public service. Such a scheme should be designed to honour excellence and pre-eminence in the field of public service delivery and have a distinctive national identify and branding.

6.5.1   Levels of achievement

Given the different bases from which organisations will be progressing, it is important that a range of levels of achievement would be recognised under the new scheme. Similarly, it would be important to encourage progression to different levels of achievement by the same body as its approach to quality customer service becomes more advanced and innovative. In accordance with best practice internationally, such an award could have three levels:

- *céim an chré-umha* (bronze level) signifying proven *commitment* to QCS throughout its approach to service delivery
- *céim an airgid* (silver level) signifying proven *achievement* in QCS throughout its approach to service delivery
- *céim an óir* (gold level) signifying proven *excellence* in QCS throughout its approach to service delivery.

In addition, the outstanding prize winner from each level of the new scheme could receive an individual prize for achievement from the Taoiseach at an annual high-profile event, attracting extensive media coverage. All those attaining bronze, silver or gold levels of achievement could be invited to attend that event to gain recognition and to facilitate networking. Similarly, all those attaining a particular level of achievement should be encouraged to include appropriate details of that award (including date of attainment) on business and other communications. To assist recognition by the external customers, and encourage a sense of achievement amongst internal customers of this level of attainment, it is suggested that an appropriate and clearly identifiable logo is designed and used for this purpose.

6.5.2 Frequency/duration of award

While the announcement of awards could occur annually, at the aforementioned event, awards could be retained by the organisation concerned for up to three years, subject to review to ensure that standards of excellence are maintained. As part of their commitment to the active promotion of QCS and continuous improvement, award winners, at all levels, could be required to participate in an annual seminar to disseminate their quality strategies to encourage less successful applicants. Likewise, successful organisations should be encouraged, on a voluntary basis, to participate in locally based or regional workshops for potential or actual applicants to share their knowledge and expertise.

6.5.3 Level of eligibility

Quality customer service is good for business and, as the

review of national and international evidence has clearly indicated, the most effective approaches to mainstreaming QCS are those that are rooted in every aspect of the way in which that business is undertaken. Clearly it is difficult to be definitive in this matter, given the size and complexity of the Irish public service and its constituent parts. However, it is envisaged that applications for recognition under the new scheme would come from individual business units and teams of staff providing specific goods or services primarily to external customers. Such business units could include sections of government departments and local authorities (including local or district offices), Garda stations, schools, health centres or operational units within hospitals, state-sponsored companies and so on. While such a scheme is most likely to attract non-commercial public service organisations, there would appear to be no reason why it could not also prove attractive to commercial public sector companies.

6.5.4   Coverage
Geographically, it is assumed that participation in the new scheme would be confined to Irish public bodies. However, participation might be attractive to the small number of international institutions operating within the State. Additionally, engagement with the scheme could prove attractive for cross-border initiatives.

6.5.5   Prestige of award
To attract wide-spread participation and motivate management and staff alike to engage seriously with the challenges presented by mainstreaming QCS in their business planning and processes, it is vitally important that attainment of the new award is a prestigious achievement at bronze, silver or gold levels. This prestige could be signified by the endorsement of the Taoiseach at the awards ceremony, and consequential media coverage, but could only be assured by the objectivity and impartiality of the award process itself.

6.5.6   Process
In accordance with experience gained from other QCS

accreditation and recognition schemes, it is suggested that recognition under the new scheme could follow a multiphase process. All business units might undergo an initial self-assessment process, prior to formal application for official accreditation. The formal application process to the new scheme could then involve successful completion of a detailed application form (together with supporting evidence and documentation), external assessment by an objective third-party (formally trained for that task), a site visit and discussion of the application with participants, a supportive but critical feedback report and an award or commendation depending upon the assessment outcome. Given the importance of the outcome of the assessment process for the organisations involved, it would be critically important to the integrity of the scheme and its administration that assessment would be based upon clearly understood and applicable criteria. While applications for participation in the scheme could be made throughout the calendar year, it is suggested that, for logistical purposes, assessments would be organised, at least initially, on a quarterly basis to stagger the workload.

6.5.7 Assessment Criteria

As previously indicated, the recently approved Guiding Principles for the preparation of departmental Customer Service Action Plans, and the roll-out of the QCS Initiative to the wider public service, would appear to provide a good initial basis for the common assessment of business units under the new scheme. These twelve principles provide a common basis for assessment across the public service, although their implications for individual sectors and business units within their sectors will of course vary.

As we saw in our review of existing national and international schemes, scores and weightings are frequently given to assist the assessment of achievement against evaluative criteria. A similar approach is suggested here, with a maximum of up to ten points to be awarded on independent assessment for proven achievement under each of the following twelve criteria[9]:

- quality standards (10 points)
- equality/diversity (10 points)
- physical access (10 points)
- information (10 points)
- timeliness and courtesy (10 points)
- complaints (10 points)
- appeals (10 points)
- consultation and evaluation (10 points)
- choice (10 points)
- official languages equality (10 points)
- better co-ordination (10 points)
- internal customer (10 points).

In this regard, it is important to note that the new scheme is envisaged as being complementary to, rather than competitive with, other accreditation schemes currently in operation, e.g. ISO 9000 and EFQM. It is anticipated that the new scheme could build upon existing experience with light frameworks, such as the CAF, and provide a significant stepping stone towards accreditation under more comprehensive high-level accreditation frameworks like the EFQM (see Chapters Three and Five). For this reason, it is important that the assessment criteria include issues such as leadership, strategy and planning, and investment in people, which are characteristic of higher-level frameworks like EFQM.

Accordingly in the light of best practice internationally, scores should be given for proven evidence of action taken under three additional categories:

- leadership (10 points)
- strategy and planning (10 points)
- investment in people (10 points).

Such an arrangement would result in a maximum achievable score of 150 points, with indicative ranges for each level of achievement being, for example:

- *céim an chré-umha* (bronze level): 80-110 points
- *céim an airgid* (silver level): 111-130 points
- *céim an óir* (gold level): 131-150 points.

It is, however, suggested that scoring ranges are not finalised for the scheme until they have been pilot tested in a variety of business unit types prior to the formal invitation of applications. Detailed guidelines would also need to be prepared centrally to guide the assessment process and to optimise consistency across the scheme. To assist thinking in this area, examples of the types of achievement to be sought under a number of the categories are given below. Finally, it must be noted that by attributing maximum scores in this way equally across all fifteen evaluative criteria, each criterion is effectively being given an equal weighting. Further consideration would need to be given to the desirability or otherwise of this approach, perhaps following the piloting phase.

6.5.8 Assessment examples

As a bottom line, to achieve a minimum score of five points under each category it is assumed that, for example, each of the specific points identified under the Guiding Principles has been meaningfully addressed (see Appendix 1). We provide here some examples to illustrate the types of initiative that could be expected under the evaluative criteria.

- *Leadership*
  Management must demonstrate its commitment and give visible leadership in making quality customer service a priority objective. Such leadership could be demonstrated by continued personal involvement in staff meetings to develop QCS initiatives, regular face-to-face contact with external customers, demonstrating practical support to front-line staff and providing real support and encouragement to business units seeking recognition under the new scheme.

- *Investment in people*
  Achievement under this category would be additional to that under the Internal Customer (see Appendix 1). Evidence here could be sought of undertaking QCS training programmes to meet specific needs, whether it be awareness raising for all staff, specific skills for

frontline staff or change management skills training for middle managers. Evidence of training needs analysis, prior to such an undertaking, could also be sought, together with clear indications of action taken to follow up the training initiatives. Involvement with staff exchange programmes to facilitate the sharing of best practice could also be a useful indicator of proactive investment in people. Active support for staff dealing directly with QCS issues could be sought. Involvement in wider schemes such as *Excellence through People* could also be a useful indicator of such commitment (see FÁS, 1998). Details of the equivalent UK scheme are provided at Appendix 2 for comparative purposes.

- *Quality standards*
Clearly, the development of standards should be specific to the particular business involved. However, certain common approaches could be expected. Such standards should be explicit, simple, meaningful, challenging and progressive over time. They should also be developed in close collaboration with those required to deliver them. For illustrative purposes, examples of service standards set for UK central government departments and agencies are given at Appendix 3. Details are also provided there of specific standards set by the Inland Revenue and Benefits Agency because of their potential relevance to the equivalent Irish departments/offices. The types of performance indicators used by local authorities in the UK are also reported in Appendix 3 for consideration. Best practice also requires the involvement of customers themselves in the setting of service standards. Details of Canadian experience with such an approach is reported in Appendix 4 for illustrative purposes.

- *Information*
Public servants often over estimate, or give insufficient regard to, the variations in levels of literacy in the national adult population. This is a particularly important issue when providing services to socially or educationally disadvantaged groups.

For example, a recent OECD-wide survey indicated that 25 per cent of the Irish population were only capable of performing the most simple literary tasks, i.e. locating a single piece of information in a text where there is not distracting information and where the structure of the text assists the search (see Department of Education, 1997). How many public service informational documents would meet that criterion? Accordingly, undertaking a planned programme of revision of information material for the general public, along the lines advocated by the Plain English Campaign (2000)[10], could be taken as concrete evidence of adopting a proactive stance on this important social inclusion issue. Similarly, the important emphasis contained within the new principles on the effective use of internet and IT-based services cannot ignore the risk of an information underclass developing where, for a variety of reasons, significant sections of the community are excluded from these technologies. Assessors could consider evidence of sensitivity and responsiveness to such issues in their evaluations.

- *Timeliness and courtesy*
  In addition to setting, monitoring and improving specific standards in this area, evidence could be sought on the operationalisation by all staff in their treatment of internal and external customers of *Public Bodies and the Citizen: The Ombudsman's Guide to Standards of Best Practice for Public Servants*. While this would also need to be addressed under the complaints and appeals categories, saying 'sorry' when there has been an error or someone has been unnecessarily caused distress can be taken as a useful indicator of the courtesy and respect afforded to customers.

These examples would need to be developed further by officials as part of the preparation for the introduction of the scheme in due course. Similarly, the supporting documentation for the final scheme will also need to include examples for the remaining ten evaluative criteria.

6.5.9   Funding

While it has been possible to identify the types of administrative charges made to applicants and participants under existing schemes (see Chapter Three), it has proved extremely difficult to obtain comprehensive costings of the types of budget required to launch and sustain a scheme such as that envisaged. For example, partial costings for the Charter Mark initiative (see Chapter Three) are only available on a UK-wide basis. Likewise, it is outside the scope of this study to estimate the net costs of the proposed scheme to the exchequer, given the potential savings to be achieved from improved business practices by public bodies.

However, one possible scenario is as follows. Initial development costs to launch the scheme could be covered by the Change Management Budget (2001), with specific provision being made for the first year of the scheme in subsequent budgets. The possibility of partial private sector sponsorship for such a scheme could merit consideration. In this regard, it is interesting to note that the recently launched *Levels of Excellence Scheme for the Northern Ireland Public Sector* is resourced in part from a major private sector company. At a minimum, the Irish private sector might wish to sponsor the annual awards for outstanding performance at each of the three levels of the scheme. We also suggest that if attainment of an award level is associated with a financial prize, then that reward could be donated to a (local) registered charity nominated by the winning team. Such an approach could provide a further tangible link between the development and promotion of QCS with the wider civic responsibility of public service providers.

On-going scheme costs could be partially defrayed by charging for participation in the scheme. However, consideration should be given to the wisdom of charging, including the level of charges, when the objective is to encourage optimal participation by business units and functional teams of staff across the public service. For example, it might be desirable to seek comparatively low charges for the first three years of the scheme to assist its launch and consolidation. Likewise, whatever the level of charges agreed, it could be desirable to provide the initial self-assessment phase on a no-charge basis.

6.5.10 Management and administration
Subject to oversight, monitoring and performance review at central government level, responsibility for the management and operation of the new scheme could be outsourced to an independent agency with the appropriate skills and competencies to undertake this important and high-profile task. This project could be awarded following a competitive tendering exercise on a contractual basis for three years, in the first instance, subject to satisfactory annual review. The operation of the scheme itself, in its entirety, could in turn be the subject of internal and external review at the end of each three year period, in advance of subsequent contractual renewal.

6.5.11 Going forward
To help inform the debate, a QCS Mark for the Irish public service has been outlined above to reflect best practice in Ireland and overseas. The proposal is also informed by the views obtained from a range of key informants during the course of this research. In accordance with good practice, however, it should also be treated as a draft scheme which could itself be subject to revision, refinement and further articulation in the light of informed customer feedback. Assuming that a QCS scheme is approved in due course, further detailed development work would also be necessary to ensure that the administrative and support structures would be in place to allow the initial self-assessment phase and first applications to be received at the earlierst opportunity.

6.6 Concluding remarks
A QCS Mark for the Irish public service could not aspire to, nor could it practically seek to, address all the current challenges faced by public service bodies in their efforts to mainstream customer service values throughout their organisations and business processes. It should certainly

not be seen nor promoted as a panacea for present shortcomings. However, this research has shown, by drawing extensively upon international and national experiences to date, that such a scheme could make a very significant contribution to taking the next phase of the QCS Initiative forward in a meaningful way. Above all, if properly introduced and managed, it could result in significant improvements in the quality of services provided to the public, as well as significant improvements in the recognition and morale of those providing those services.

The introduction of a QCS accreditation and recognition system for the Irish public service could be the beginning of a new phase of continuous improvement. It would certainly not be an end in itself. In a recent report from the New Zealand government, which assessed the responsiveness of five services to the needs of clients, the following concluding remarks were made. 'Continuous improvement is the systematic process which seeks to identify opportunities to improve service. ... For the purpose of seeking continuous improvement, a client-focused organisation will:

- systematically seek opportunities to improve service

- identify the potential to improve work processes which have a service impact

- use service 'champions' to lead and promote continuous improvement

- seek opportunities to learn from benchmarking studies of comparable organisations and processes

- build ongoing relationships with external stakeholders as a means of obtaining valuable feedback on service awareness and quality

- recognise that community groups can provide valuable representation for clients, and are a valuable source of information about how its services are received.'

At present, there are champions of quality customer service in all sectors of the Irish public service and at all levels of staff within a multiplicity of organisations. Such champions have little recognition, either formal or otherwise, of the vital work they do. A well-designed QCS Mark scheme could both provide a means of acknowledging that achievement, encouraging its far greater development, and provide a valuable tool for organisations of all sizes to embark upon a meaningful programme of continuous quality improvement.

1. In addition to representatives of government departments and offices, the current QCS Working Group includes representatives from the Northern Ireland Civil Service – Public Service Improvement Unit, the Consumers Association, the Irish National Organisation for the Unemployed, the Disability Federation, the Small Firms Association, the Equality Authority, the National Consultative Committee on Racism and Interculturalism, the Federated Union of Government Employees, the Public Service Executive Union, IMPACT, the Civil and Public Service Union, the Institute of Public Administration, REACH and Comhdháil Náisiúnta na Gaelige.

2. The Irish public service comprises the civil service, An Garda Síochána, the Defence Forces, education (excluding private institutions), health services (excluding private institutions), local authorities and non-commercial state-sponsored bodies. The public sector comprises the public service plus the commercial state-sponsored bodies (see Humphreys and Gorman, 1987 and Humphreys, 1983).

3. In addition to those considered in detail here, it is also important to note public service quality awards introduced in other countries. These include *The Hellenic Quality Award System* (Greece); *Premio Innovazione nella Pubblica Amministrazione Cento Progetti* (Italy); the *Public Service Quality Contest* (Portugal) and the *Kronorna bland verken* (Sweden).

4. The Equal Status Act (2000) outlaws discrimination in the following areas:
   - disposal of goods
   - provision of services and facilities
   - disposal of premises
   - provision of accommodation
   - participation in educational establishments
   - participation in clubs.

5. The departments and offices in question are: Agriculture, Food and Rural Development; Arts,

Heritage, Gaeltacht and the Islands; Central Statistics Office; Civil Service and Local Appointments Commissioners; Defence; Education and Science; Enterprise, Trade and Employment; Environment and Local Government; Finance; Foreign Affairs; Health and Children; Justice, Equality and Law Reform; Land Registry; Marine and Natural Resources; Met Éireann; Ordnance Survey; Public Enterprise; Public Works (including Government Supplies Agency); Revenue Commissioners; Social Community and Family Affairs; Taoiseach; Tourism, Sport and Recreation; Valuation.

6. REACH is a cross-departmental agency established by government to improve the quality of service to customers of the Irish public service. In particular, it will develop the framework for the integration of services and the implementation of e-government in Ireland. The systems developed by REACH will aim to:

- integrate services – customers will access a range of related services through a single access point
- personalise services to the individual needs of the customer and his or her preferences
- provide choice and convenience – customers will choose the access channel and time of access which best suit them
- reduce and eliminate repetitive form filling and repeated provision of basic personal data
- simplify services in terms of accessibility of information and application processes to allow for self-service access by customers over the Internet.

As a first-step, self-service information systems are being developed for personal customers (OASIS – Comhairle) and for businesses (BASIS – Department of Enterprise, Trade and Employment). REACH will report to government through the Minister for Social, Community and Family Affairs and will be developed in close collaboration with the Departments of an Taoiseach and Finance, which have specific responsibil-ities for the IS Action Plan and e-government strategies respectively. For further details see www.reach.ie.

7. In March 2000, there were an estimated 75,000 hits to the government website with the larger departments having upwards of 15,000 hits per month.

8. The following sectoral level performance indicators have been agreed for QCS:

   • departments and offices to update and publish new three year Customer Service Action Plans incorporating performance indicators (April 2001)

   • departments and offices to consult with their customers – internal and external – on the development, delivery and review of services (April 2001 and ongoing)

   • departments and offices to embed their plan in strategy statements, business planning and the Performance Management Development System (PMDS) processes (October 2001 and ongoing).

   • departments and offices to report progress in the annual progress report

   • relevant departments and offices to take meaningful steps to extend the revised QCS principles to the wider public service bodies for which they have responsibility (April 2001)

   • departments and offices to ensure meaningful evaluation of their service delivery (ongoing).

9. For simplicity it is proposed, at least initially, that calculations will be based on integers rather than decimal or fractional scores.

10. While UK-based, this pioneering movement has made available a number of excellent guidance documents on its website at http://www.plainenglish.co.uk. These include: *How to write letters in plain English, How to write reports in plain English* and *An A to Z of Alternative Words*. Equivalent disciplines for the use of plain language need to be exercised in the use of Irish in informational material provided by public service bodies.

Ahern, B. (1999), 'Delivering Quality Public Services – responding to the needs of a changing environment', *Link – Newsletter of the Strategic Management Initiative,* July, Dublin: Department of the Taoiseach

All-Party Oireachtas Committee on the Strategic Management Initiative (1999), *Quality Customer Service in the Department of Agriculture and Food,* First Report, Department of the Taoiseach, Dublin: Stationery Office

All-Party Oireachtas Committee on the Strategic Management Initiative (1999), *Quality Customer Service in the Sea Fishing Sector in the Department of the Marine and Natural Resources,* Second Report, Department of the Taoiseach, Dublin: Stationery Office

Arnstein, S.R. (1969), 'Ladder of citizen participation', *American Institute of Planners Journal,* July 1969, pp. 216-224

Aspects of Excellence European Quality Award report (1999), p8, The *EFQM Excellence Model an evolution not a revolution,* London: European Quality Publications Ltd

Australian Quality Council (2000), *Australian Quality Council – Our Business,* http:// www.aqc.org.au/ob-intro.htm/

Bendell, T., L. Boulter and J. Kelly (1994), *Implementing Quality in the Public Sector,* London: Pitman

Better Local Government: *A Programme for Change (1996),* Department of the Environment and Local Government, Dublin: Stationery Office

Boyle, R. (1989), *Managing Public Sector Performance: A comparative study of performance measurement systems in the public and private sectors,* Dublin: Institute of Public Administration

Boyle, R. (1996), *Measuring Civil Service Performance,* Dublin: Institute of Public Administration

Bywater (1991), *The Bywater Total Quality Management Strategy Package,* Surrey: Bywater Plc

Cabinet Office (1998), *Service First: The New Charter Programme, How to apply for a Charter Mark 1999,* London: Cabinet Office

Cabinet Office (1999), *Service First: A guide to quality schemes for the public sector,* London: Cabinet Office

Cabinet Office (1999), *Service First: The New Charter Programme, How to apply for a Charter Mark 2000,* London: Cabinet Office

Cabinet Office (2000), *The Charter Mark Guide for Applicants*, London: Cabinet Office

CCMD (1999), *Citizen-Centred Services: Responding to the needs of Canadians*, Canadian Centre for Management Development: http://www.ccmd-ccg.gc.ca

Claver, E., J. Llopis, J. L. Gascó, H. Molina, F. J. Conca (1999), 'Public Administration: From Bureaucratic Culture To Citizen-Oriented Culture', *The International Journal of Public Sector Management* 12(5), pp. 455-464

Curry, A. and D. Herbert, (1998), 'Continuous improvement in public services – a way forward', *Managing Service Quality* 8 (5), pp. 339-349

Delivering Better Government (1996), Second Report to Government of the Co-ordinating Group of Secretaries, A Programme of Change for the Irish Civil Service, Dublin: Stationery Office

Delivering Better Local Government (1996), Department of the Environment and Local Government, Dublin: Stationery Office

Denmark (1998), *Examples of initiatives in performance management and public service delivery, the Danish Public Sector Quality Award*, http://www.oecd.org/puma/focus/compend/denmark/perfman.htm

Denmark (2000), 'Public Management developments in Denmark: Update 2000-1', *Performance Management and Service Delivery, The Quality Award for the Public Sector*, http://www.oecd.org/puma/country/surveys2000/surv2000dk.htm

Department of Education (1997), *International Adult Literacy Survey: Results for Ireland*, Dublin: Stationery Office

Department of the Environment, Transport and Regions (2000), *Guide to Equality Schemes and Best Value*, London

Department of the Environment and Local Government (2000), *Modernising Government – the Challenge for Local Government*, Dublin: The Stationery Office

Dewhurst, F., A.R. Martinez-Lorente, B.J. Dale (1999), 'TQM in public organisations: an examination of the issues', *Managing Service Quality*, Vol. 9, No. 4, MCB University Press

Donnelly, M. (1999), 'Making the difference: quality strategy in the public sector', *Managing Service Quality*, Vol. 9, No. 1, MCB University Press

Edvardsson, B. (1998), 'Service Quality Improvement', *Managing Service Quality*, Vol. 8, No. 2, MCB University Press

EFQM (1999a), *Introducing Excellence*, Brussels: EFQM.

EFQM (1999b), *The EFQM in action*, Brussels: EFQM.

EFQM (1999c), *Eight Fundamentals of Excellence, The Fundamental Concepts and their Benefits*, Brussels: EFQM.

EFQM (1999d), *EFQM Excellence Model, Public and Voluntary Sector Version*, http:// www.efqm.org/le99/changesps. htm

EFQM (1999e), 'Quality Link', *EFQM Newsletter Vol. 11*, No. 59, Brussels: EFQM

EFQM (1999f), *Radar and the EFQM Excellence Model*, Brussels: EFQM

Equality Authority (1999), *Customer Service Action Plan*, Dublin: EA

EIPA (2000), *CAF Common Assessment Framework*, circulated at European Union International Conference on Best Practice, Lisbon

European Organisation for Quality and the Centre for Excellence-Finland (2000), *Towards a European Vision of Quality – The Way Forward*

Excellence Ireland (1999), 'EFQM releases new excellence model', p. 8, 'Lessons from an SME pilot', *Best Practice*, May 1999, Dublin: Best Practice

Excellence Ireland (1999), 'Improved EFQM Excellence Model', *Best Practice*, October 1999, Dublin: Best Practice

Excellence Ireland (1999), *The Q-Mark based on Business Excellence*, Dublin: Excellence Ireland.

FÁS (1998), *Excellence through People: Guidelines for Self Assessment and Application Form*, Dublin: FÁS.

Garda Síochána (1998), *Quality Customer Service Action Plan: Putting People First*, Dublin: Stationery Office

Gaster, L. (1999), 'Quality Management in Local Government – Issues and Experiences', *Public Policy and Administration* 14 (3), pp. 35-55

Groth, J.C. and R.T. Dye (1999), 'Service quality: perceived value, expectations, shortfalls, and bonuses', *Managing Service Quality* 9(4), pp. 274-285

Guidelines on Planning for Quality Customer Service: SMI Quality Customer Service Working Group and Front-line Group, June 1997, Dublin: Department of the Taoiseach

Ham, C.J. (1980), 'Community Health Council participation in the NHS planning system', *Social Policy and Administration* 14(3) Autumn 1980

Humphreys, P.C. (1983), *Public Service Employment: An Examination of Strategies in Ireland and Other European Countries*, Dublin: Institute of Public Administration

Humphreys, P.C. (1998), *Improving Public Service Delivery*, CPMR Discussion Paper No. 7, Dublin: Institute of Public Administration

Humphreys, P.C. and P. Gorman (1987), *Information on Public Sector Employment and Manpower*, Dublin: Institute of Public Administration

Humphreys, P.C., S. Fleming and O. O'Donnell (1999), *Improving Public Services in Ireland: A Case-Study Approach*, CPMR Discussion Paper No. 11, Dublin: Institute of Public Administration

Humphreys, P.C. and M. Worth-Butler, (1999), *Key Human Resource Management Issues in the Irish Public* Service, CPMR Discussion Paper No. 10, Dublin: Institute of Public Administration

Irish Marketing Surveys (1997), Survey of Civil Service Customers, Dublin: Department of the Taoiseach.

Investors in People (2000), www.iipuk.co.uk

Kano, N. and H. Gitlow (1988-89), Lectures in quality control and the Deming method of quality improvement, University of Miami Institute for the Study of Quality in Manufacturing and Service. Unpublished lecture notes quoted in Milakovich (1992)

Keegan, R. (ed) (1998), *Benchmarking FACTS: A European Perspective*, Brussels: European Company Benchmarking Forum

Kuuttiniemi, K. and P. Virtanen (1998), *Citizen's Charters and Compensation Mechanisms*, Research Report 11/98, Helsinki: Ministry of Finance

Leahy, A.L. (1998), 'Moving to a Quality Culture', in Leahy, A.L., and M. Wiley (eds) (1998), *The Irish Health System in the 21st Century*, Dublin: Oak Tree Press

McCumiskey, E. (1992), *Quality in the Civil Service*, Presentation at the Irish Quality Association/Institute of Public Administration conference on Public Service Quality

Milakovich, M.E. (1992), 'Total Quality Management for Public Service Productivity Improvement', in Holzer, M. (ed) (1992), *Public Productivity Handbook*, New York: Marcel Dekker Inc

National Economic and Social Forum (1995), *Quality Delivery of Social Services*, Report No. 6, Dublin: NESF

National Quality Institute (1997), 'Achieving Citizen/Client focused service delivery', *A Framework for Effective public service organisations – Canadian Quality Criteria for the Public Sector*, Canada: NQI

National Institute of Standards and Technology, *The Malcolm Baldrige National Quality Award*, http:// www. quality.nist.gov

National Institute of Standards and Technology, *Baldrige Criteria for Performance Excellence 2000*, http:// www.quality.nist.gov/bcpg.pdf.htm

National Performance Review (1997), 'Putting Customers First '97', *Standards for Serving the American People*, http: //www.npr.gov/custtserv/1997/chapter1.htm/

National Performance Review (2000), *Frequently Asked Questions about the National Partnership for Reinventing Government*, http://www.npr.gov/library/papers/ bkgrd/q-n-a.htm/

New Zealand Quality Foundation (2000), *New Zealand Quality Foundation Awards, New Zealand National Awards and the New Zealand Business Excellence Awards*, http://www.nzquality.org.nz

NSAI (1999), *ISO 9000 Quality for Health Services*, NSAI/Health Services Joint Working Group, Dublin: NSAI

OECD (1994), *Service Quality Initiatives in OECD Member Countries*, Background paper prepared by Public Management (PUMA) Secretariat for symposium in OECD, Paris, 7-8 November

OECD (1996), *Responsive Government: Service Quality Initiatives*, Paris: OECD

OECD (2000), *Public Management Developments in Finland: Update 2000*, Performance Management and Services delivery – Finnish Quality Award competition, http:// www.oecd.org/ puma/country/Surveys2000/surv 2000 fi.htm

Ovretveit, J. (1991), *Health Service Quality: An introduction to quality methods for health services*, Oxford: Blackwell Special Projects

Plain English Campaign (2000), http://www.plainenglish.co.uk

Potter, J. (1988), 'Consumerism and the public sector: How well does the coat fit?', *Public Administration*, 66 Summer, pp. 149-164

Pounder, J.S. (2000), 'Evaluating the Relevance of Quality to Institutional Performance Assessment in Higher Education', *Evaluation* 6(1), pp. 66-78

Programme for Prosperity and Fairness (2000), Dublin: Stationery Office

Public Bodies and the Citizen – The Ombudsman's Guide to Standards of Best Practice for Public Servants (1997), Dublin: Office of the Ombudsman

Rothery, B. (1996), *ISO 9000 Second Edition*, Hampshire: Gower Publishing Ltd

Seddon, J. (1997), *In Pursuit of Quality, The Case against ISO 9000*, Dublin: Oak Tree Press

Serving the Country Better (1985), White Paper on the Public Service, Dublin: Stationery Office

Shand, D. and M. Arnberg (1996), Background Paper, in OECD (1996) *Responsive Government: Service Quality Initiatives*, Paris: OECD

Shaping a Healthier Future (1994), Department of Health, Dublin: Stationery Office

Shaw, C.D. (1986), Introducing Quality Assurance, *Kings Fund Project Paper No. 64*, London: Kings Fund

Stewart, J. and M. Clarke, (1987), 'The Public service orientation: issues and dilemmas', *Public Administration*, 65(3), pp. 161-167

Speyer Quality Award, Information in English, http://www.hfv-speyer.de/5-speyerer-qualitaetswettbewerb-2000/10.htm

Speyer Quality Award, Information in French, http://www.dhv-speyer.de/5-speyerer-qualitaetswettbewerb-2000/franzosisch.htm

Townsend, P. and J. Gebhart (1986), *Commit to Quality*, New York: Wiley

United States Office of Personnel Management (2000), *The President's Quality Award Program 2000 Information and Application*, Washington: United States Office of Personnel Management, www.opm.gov/quality/ pqa00.doc

United States Office of Personnel Management (2000), *The President's Quality Award Program*, www.opm.gov/quality/index.htm

Walsh, K. (1991), 'Quality and Public Services'. *Public Administration*, No. 69, Oxford: Blackhall, Winter, pp. 503-514

APPENDIX 1

Revised Quality Customer Service (QCS) Principles for Customer Action Plans (2001-2004)

At its meeting (19 July 2000), the government agreed the following revised QCS principles. These principles are to be given full effect by departments and offices as they proceed to update, refine and publish their new customer action plans by the first quarter of 2001 and to ensure continuous quality improvement.

The principles are as follows:

1. *Quality Service Standards:*
   Publish a statement that outlines the nature and quality of service which customers can expect, and display it prominently at the point of service delivery.

2. *Equality/Diversity*
   Ensure the rights to equal treatment established by equality legislation, and accommodate diversity, so as to contribute to equality for the groups covered by the equality legislation (under the grounds of gender, marital status, family status, sexual orientation, religious belief, age, disability, race and membership of the Traveller community).

   Identify and work to eliminate barriers to access to services for people experiencing poverty and social exclusion, and for those facing geographic barriers to services.

3. *Physical Access*
   Provide clean, accessible public offices, which ensure privacy, comply with occupational and safety standards and, as part of this, facilitate access for people with disabilities and others with specific needs.

4. *Information*
   Take a pro-active approach in providing information that is clear, timely and accurate, is available at all points of contact and meets the requirements of people with specific needs. Ensure that the potential offered by Information Technology is fully availed of and that the information available on public service websites follows the guidelines on web publication. Continue to drive for

simplification of rules, regulations, forms, information leaflets and procedures.

5. *Timeliness and Courtesy*
Deliver quality services with courtesy, sensitivity and the minimum delay, fostering a climate of mutual respect between provider and customer. Give contact names in all communications to ensure ease of ongoing transactions.

6. *Complaints*
Maintain a well-publicised, accessible, transparent and simple-to-use system of dealing with complaints about the quality of service provided.

7. *Appeals*
Similarly, maintain a formalised, well-publicised, accessible, transparent and simple-to-use system of appeal/review for customers who are dissatisfied with decisions in relation to services.

8. *Consultation and Evaluation*
Provide a structured approach to meaningful consultation with, and participation by, the customer in relation to the development, delivery and review of services. Ensure meaningful evaluation of service delivery.

9. *Choice*
Provide choice, where feasible, in service delivery including payment methods, location of contact points, opening hours and delivery times. Use available and emerging technologies to ensure maximum access and choice, and quality of delivery.

10. *Official Languages Equality*
Provide quality services through Irish and/or bilingually and inform customers of their rights to choose to be dealt with through one or other of the official languages.

11. *Better Co-ordination*
Foster a more co-ordinated and integrated approach to delivery of public services.

12. *Internal Customer*
Ensure staff are recognised as internal customers and that they are properly supported and consulted with regard to service delivery issues.

APPENDIX 2

Investors in People National Standard

Principles	Indicators	Evidence
Commitment An Investor in People is fully committed to developing its people in order to achieve its aims and objectives	**1. The organisation is committed to supporting the development of its people**	▪ Top management can describe strategies that they have put in place to support the development of people in order to improve the organisation's performance ▪ Managers can describe specific actions that they have taken and are currently taking to support the development of people ▪ People can confirm that the specific strategies and actions described by top management and managers take place ▪ People believe the organisation is genuinely committed to supporting their development
	2. People are encouraged to improve their own and other people's performance	▪ People can give examples of how they have been encouraged to improve their own performance ▪ People can give examples of how they have been encouraged to improve other people's performance
	3. People believe their contribution to the organisation is recognised	▪ People can describe how their contribution to the organisation is recognised ▪ People believe that their contribution to the organisation is recognised ▪ People receive appropriate and constructive feedback on a timely and regular basis
	4. The organisation is committed to ensuring equality of opportunity in the development of its people	▪ Top management can describe strategies that they have put in place to ensure equality of opportunity in the development of people ▪ Managers can describe specific actions that they have taken and are currently taking to ensure equality of opportunity in the development of people ▪ People confirm that the specific strategies and actions described by top management and managers take place and recognise the needs of different groups ▪ People believe the organisation is genuinely committed to ensuring equality of opportunity in the development of people

105

Principles	Indicators	Evidence
Planning An Investor in People is clear about its aims and its objectives and what its people need to do to achieve them	5. **The organisation has a plan with clear aims and objectives which are understood by everyone**	▪ The organisation has a plan with clear aims and objectives ▪ People can consistently explain the aims and objectives of the organisation at a level appropriate to their role ▪ Representative groups are consulted about the organisation's aims and objectives
	6. **The development of people is in line with the organisation's aims and objectives**	▪ The organisation has clear priorities which link the development of people to its aims and objectives at organisation, team and individual level ▪ People clearly understand what their development activities should achieve, both for them and the organisation
	7. **People understand how they contribute to achieving the organisation's aims and objectives**	▪ People can explain how they contribute to achieving the organisation's aims and objectives
Action An Investor in People develops its people effectively in order to improve its performance	8. **Managers are effective in supporting the development of people**	▪ The organisation makes sure that managers have the knowledge and skills they need to develop their people ▪ Managers at all levels understand what they need to do to support the development of people ▪ People understand what their manager should be doing to support their development ▪ Managers at all levels can give examples of actions that they have taken and are currently taking to support the development of people ▪ People can describe how their managers are effective in supporting their development

	9. People learn and develop effectively	▪ People who are new to the organisation, and those new to a job, can confirm that they have received an effective induction ▪ The organisation can show that people learn and develop effectively ▪ People can give examples of what they have learnt (knowledge, skills and attitude) from development activities ▪ Development is linked to relevant external qualifications and standards (or both) where appropriate
Principles	**Indicators**	**Evidence**
Evaluation An Investor in People understands the impact of its investment in people on its performance	10. The development of people improves the performance of the organisation	▪ The organisation can show that the development of people has improved the performance of the organisation, teams and individuals
	11. People understand the impact of the development of people on the performance of the organisation, teams and individuals	▪ Top management understands the overall costs and benefits of the development of people and its impact on performance ▪ People can explain the impact of their development on their performance, and the performance of their team and the organisation as a whole
	12. The organisation gets better at developing its people	▪ People can give examples of relevant and timely improvements that have been made to development activities

APPENDIX 3

*Examples of quality standards used in the UK
by central government departments, executive
agencies and local government*

Overview of UK standards approach

The UK is possibly the leader in the development of service standards and targets, reflecting to a large extent its approach to managing public services – devolved responsibility within departments and to executive agencies along with mechanisms aimed at enhancing accountability. The approach taken is to clarify what should be expected of public services in national standards, and then to make organisations accountable for the delivery of these standards through regular monitoring, reporting and external scrutiny.

In 1997, six standards were introduced for central government departments and agencies, and were revised in the *Modernising Government* White Paper in 1999/2000. The six standards relate to:

- replying to letters from the public quickly and clearly, including letters, faxes, and e-mails. This includes setting a target and reporting performance against the target

- seeing people within ten minutes of any appointment made. In addition, each department and agency must set a target for seeing people without an appointment, and publish performance against the target

- answering telephone calls quickly and helpfully. Each department and agency is required to set a target for answering calls to telephone enquiry points and publishing performance against this target

- providing clear and straightforward information about its services and those of related services providers, including telephone enquiry numbers and e-mail addresses. The target is to have at least one e-mail address for handling enquiries

- having a complaints procedure, publicising it, including publication on the Internet, and sending information about it to customers who request it

- doing everything reasonably possible to make all services available to everyone, including people with special needs; consulting users and potential users regularly about the service and reporting on the result.

Figure One: Central government and agency
performance targets 1999/2000

Standard	Target set
Responding to correspondence	Between 3 and 20 days 1 dept – 3 days 11 depts – 10 days 14 depts – 15 days 1 dept – 18 days 13 depts – 20 days The average number of days is 15
Maximum time waiting with and without an appointment	- Standard is set at 10 minutes nationally for callers with appointments - For callers without an appointment targets are between 5 and 20 minutes. Most departments going for 10 minutes
Answering calls to designated telephone enquiry points	Number of rings / seconds before answered
E-mail enquiry points	To have at least one e-mail enquiry point

Review of Charter Standards set by Inland Revenue and the Benefits Agency

In addition, individual public bodies have initiated their own charters which include explicit commitments to improving quality standards. Two examples are cited here for illustrative purposes.

Category	Inland Revenue	Benefits Agency
Contact details	• Office opening hours • Telephone service hours • Contact details	• Types of offices, range of opening hours, where to find information on offices and types of benefit • Opening hours and switchboard hours for main offices • Internet address • Standards for telephone answering to be set by each office and displayed • Specific help lines and contact details listed
Service standards	• Answer telephone within thirty seconds at switchboard and connect to the right extension first time • See visitors without an appointment within fifteen minutes of arrival • Respond to every question or issue raised in writing within twenty-eight calendar days – where not possible will explain and when reply to be expected For all contacts we will: • Provide a clear, accurate and helpful response • Make clear what action customer needs to take next, and by what date • Give staff names • Be courteous and professional • Get every aspect of your affairs right first time by making full and correct use of information available to us • Deal with your repayment claims sent to our specialist repayment offices within twenty-eight calendar days	We will help you by: • Dealing with your claim as quickly as possible and keeping you informed about progress and decisions • Number of days to expect for decisions on different types of claims or changes in circumstances listed • Number of days can expect for response to correspondence, and explain if cannot do so • Being polite and easy to talk to • Staff to wear name badges • Giving you accurate benefit advice and information including help with applying for child support when needed • Being fair – your race, ethnic origin, age, gender, sexual orientation, religious beliefs or any disability you have will not effect how we treat you • Asking for your views and using them to give you the service you want • See callers with ten minutes of arrival, or within thirty minutes at busy times, callers with appointments within ten minutes • Provide full range of leaflets and other information, staff to give accurate information and advice based on the information given to them, information leaflets in different languages, Braille and audio cassette
Specific targets and reporting performance	• Annual customer service leaflets showing performance against the previous years targets and the targets for the current year • Information also in annual report	• Local charters also and reporting on performance against local targets

Privacy and confidentiality	• Handle affairs on a strictly confidential basis within the law • Respect privacy • Provide private room if preferred	• Only pass on information to other departments within the law
Special needs	• Provide whatever help reasonably can to cater for special needs • Visits can be arranged where not possible to visit the office	• Textphone, can request response to correspondence in Braille, audio cassette or computer disk • Can arrange to have an interpreter by appointment • Can arrange help on filling out forms if needed • Many offices have staff with some sign language skills, can arrange a British Sign Language interpreter usually within one working day • Home visit can be arranged if cannot get into the office
Legal rights and code of practice	• Own code of practice setting out approach and procedures, legal rights of customer and of Inland Revenue, explain what customer can expect to happen • Availability of copies	• Following the rules of the Social Security and Data Protection Acts and the principles of Open Government
Customers' responsibilities	• Response required to information requests • Details required when contacting the office • Need to inform office of changes in personal circumstances • Records required by law	• Giving complete and accurate information • Informing about changes in circumstance • Details required when contacting the office • Providing some means of identification
Appeals	• What to do if the customer disagrees with the Inland Revenue • Formal appeals process	• What to do if you think we have made a mistake • Information available at offices on how to make an appeal • Role of the independent tribunal to appeal benefit set out
Complaints	• What to do if unhappy with service • Formal complaints procedure	• Staff will tell you what to do if you are unhappy with the service or your benefit • Information available at offices on how to make a complaint • How to complain
Listening to customers	• Welcome suggestions • Local and national surveys • Feedback from complaints • How to make a suggestion	• Information available at offices on how to make a comment or suggestion • Comments on charter invited with contact and e-mail address
Revision date	• Annual review and date	• Charter published in 1999 and will be reviewed in 2001

Review of performance indicators used in local government in the UK

From 31 March 2000, UK local authorities were required to publish details of their performance against Best Value

Performance Indicators (BVPIs) in the Best Value Performance Plan (BVPP). Local authorities are also required to produce data on Audit Commission Performance Indicators (ACPIs), which cover areas not included in the BVPIs. Indicators relate to: corporate health, education, social services, housing and related services, environmental services, cultural and related services and emergency services. In each category, a number of 'quality' BVPIs have been specified to explicitly reflect users' experience of services and guidance has been developed for the conduct of user satisfaction surveys.

As can be seen by reviewing the range of indicators, there are several different types of indicators, many of which relate to quality customer service – some as indicators of customer satisfaction, some which relate to the organisation of services, what is provided, access, responsiveness, equality, and the efficiency of services. Several indicators could be used in the Irish public service context.

Category A : Corporate health

Planning and performance measurement
The adoption of a Local Agenda 21 Plan by 31 December 2000

Customers and the Community
- Conforming to the Commission for Racial Equality's Standard for Local Government
- Percentage of citizens satisfied with the overall service provided by their authority
- Percentage of those making complaints happy with the handling of those complaints
- The number of complaints to an Ombudsman classified as maladministration
- The percentage turnout for local elections
- The percentage of electoral registration form "A"s returned

Management of resources
- The percentage of undisputed invoices paid within thirty days
- Proportion of Council Tax collected
- Percentage of business rates which should have been received during the year that were received

Staff development
- Percentage of senior management posts filled by women
- Proportion of working days/shifts lost to sickness absence
- Voluntary leavers as a percentage of staff in post
- Early retirements (excluding ill-health retirements) as a percentage of the total workforce
- Ill-health retirements as a percentage of the total workforce
- The number of staff declaring that they meet with the Disability Discrimination Act disability definition as a percentage of the total workforce
- Minority ethnic community staff as a percentage of the total workforce

Category A: Continued

There are then separate sets of similar indicators for police services, single-service fire services, national parks and national road authorities and joint waste disposal authorities

Corporate health ACPIs

- Number of authority's buildings open to the public
- Number of such buildings in which all public areas are suitable for and accessible to disabled people
- Number of racial incidents recorded by the authority per 100,000 population
- The percentage of racial incidents that resulted in further action
- Number of domestic violence refuge places per 10,000 population provided or supported by the authority
- Total net spending per head population

Category B: Education services (not reviewed)
Category C: Social services

Strategic objective – not reviewed

Service delivery outcome
- Intensive home care (number of households receiving per 000s population aged sixty-five or over)
- Older people aged sixty-five or over helped to live at home

Quality
- Clients receiving a review as a percentage of adult clients receiving a service
- Percentage of equipment costing less than £1,000 delivered within three weeks
- Percentage of users/carers surveyed who got help quickly
- Percentage of people getting a service who received a statement of their needs and how they will be met
- Assessments per head of population
- Users/carers surveyed who said that matters relating to race, culture or religion were noted
- Relative spend on family support

Also a number of similar ACPIs

Category D: Housing and related services

Strategic objective not reviewed

Service delivery outcome
- Energy efficiency of local authority owned dwellings
- Number of local authority dwellings receiving renovation work as proportion of those needing renovation
- Percentage of urgent repairs completed within government time limits (listed per type of repair)
- Average time taken to complete non-urgent responsive repairs

Quality
- Satisfaction of tenants of council housing with the overall service provided by their landlord (survey)

Fair Access
- Satisfaction of tenants of council housing with opportunities for participation in management and decision making in relation to housing services provided by their landlord (survey)

Housing and related services ACPIs
- Does the authority follow the Commission for Racial Equality's code of practice in rented housing?
- The percentage of repair jobs for which an appointment was both made and kept by the authority
- The percentage of all current tenants owing thirteen weeks rent at 31 March 2001
- New tenancies given to vulnerable people excluding elderly people, as a percentage of all new tenancies except those given to the elderly
- The average number of homeless households in temporary accommodation during the year in bed and breakfast accommodation
- The average length of stay in bed and breakfast accommodation

---

Category D: continued

Housing Benefit and Council Tax Benefit

Strategic objective
Whether the authority has a written and proactive strategy for combating fraud and error, which embraces specific initiatives, which is communicated regularly to all staff

---

Cost/efficiency
Average cost of handling a HB or CTB claim

Service delivery outcome
1. Average time for processing new claims
2. Average time for processing notifications and changes in circumstances
3. Percentage of renewal claims processed on time
4. Percentage of cases for which the calculation of the amount of benefit due was correct on the basis of the information available to the determination, for a sample of cases checked post-determination
5. The percentage of recoverable overpayments that were recovered in the year

---

Quality and fair access
- User satisfaction survey covering issues of accessibility, staffing (helpfulness), communications and information (understandability etc)

Category E: Environmental Services

Strategic objective – not reviewed

Service delivery outcome
Number of collections missed per 1 00,000 collections of household waste

---

Quality
- Percentage of people satisfied with cleanliness standards (survey)
- Percentage of people expressing satisfaction with a) recycling facilities, b) household waste collection and c) civic amenity sites
- Percentage of people served by a kerbside collection of recyclables or within 1 kilometre of a recycling centre

Environment ACPIs
- Percentage of highways either of a high or acceptable standard of cleanliness (inspection)
- Average time taken to remove fly-tips
- Number of public conveniences sites provided by the authority normally throughout the year

---

Transport

Cost efficiency – not reviewed

Service delivery outcome
- Condition of principal roads (specialist 'reflectograph' surveys)
- Condition of non-principal roads (specialist survey)
- Percentage of street lamps not working as planned
- Road safety – road casualty statistics
- Number of days traffic controls or road closure on traffic sensitive roads caused by local authority road works per km of traffic sensitive road
- Local bus services (vehicle kms per year)
- Local bus services (passenger journeys per year)

Quality
- Percentage of users satisfied with local provision of public transport information
- Percentage of users satisfied with local bus services

Fair access
- Total number of reported incidents of dangerous damage to roads and pavements repaired or made safe within twenty-four hours

---

Transport ACPIs
- Percentage of pedestrian crossings with facilities for disabled people
- Percentage of links of footpaths and other rights of way which were signposted where they leave the road
- Percentage of total length of footpaths and other rights of way that were easy to use by members of the public

Category E: continued

Planning

Strategic objective and cost/efficiency – not reviewed

Service delivery outcome
1. Number of advertised departures from the statutory plan approved by the authority as a percentage of total permissions granted
2. Percentage of applications determined within eight weeks
3. Average time taken to determine all applications

Quality
- Percentage of applicants and those commenting on planning applications satisfied with the service received
- Score against a checklist of planning best practice

Planning ACPIs
- Percentage of standard searches carried out within ten working days

---

Category F: Cultural and related services

Strategic objective and cost/efficiency – not reviewed

Service delivery outcomes
- Number of physical visits per head of population to public libraries

Quality
- Percentage of library users who found the book/information they wanted, or reserved it, and were satisfied with the outcome

Fair access
- Percentage of residents by targeted group satisfied with the local authority's cultural activities

Cultural and related services ACPIs
- Number of swimming pool visits per 1,000 population
- Net cost of swim per year
- Number of playgrounds and play areas provided by the authority, per 1,000 children under 12
- Percentage of these which:
  - Conform to national standards for local unequipped play areas
  - Conform to national standards for local equipped play areas
  - Conform to national standards for larger, neighbourhood equipped play areas.
- Number of museums operated or supported by the LA
- Number of those museums that are registered under the Museums and Galleries Commission registration scheme
- Number of visits/ usages and those in person to museums per 1,000 population
- Net cost per visit to museums
- Number of books and other items issued by the authority's libraries per head of population

Category G: Emergency services – not reviewed

APPENDIX 4

Exploring concepts of quality in other public sector approaches: The Canadian Public Service

The Canadian Centre for Management Development established the Citizen-Centred Service Network (CCSN) in 1997. It is made up of more than 200 service quality leaders from across Canadian federal, provincial and municipal governments. The CCSN defines citizen-centred service as service improvements rooted in citizens' and clients' priorities for improvement – organising services from their perspectives rather than the organisation's perspective.

One research initiative undertaken on behalf of the CCSN was a survey of almost 3,000 Canadians. The research also resulted in the development of *The Citizens First Service Model*, made up of five elements:

- citizens' service needs and expectations

- access to service

- service delivery

- perceptions of service quality

- citizens' priorities for development.

Access to service was explored in terms of barriers to access including difficulty finding services, difficulties with telephone access, difficulties with information and explanations, parking and travel difficulties. Citizens encountered two major barriers when trying to connect to government services. There were difficulties with the telephone service – due to busy lines, failures in voice mail or not being able to find the number in the blue pages; and difficulty obtaining accurate information – being 'bounced' from person to person, being given conflicting information or being given incorrect information.

In terms of service delivery, five 'drivers' are identified and confirmed in the analysis, which it is suggested determine whether citizens rate the service they receive as good or poor:

- timeliness
- knowledgeable, competent staff
- courtesy/comfort
- fair treatment
- outcome (getting what you need) (CCMD 1998, p. 27).

The research also attempted to establish the relative importance of the five drivers and found that timeliness may be the most important, followed by outcome and then treatment by staff.

Survey participants were also asked about what would be acceptable for eight different standards and the results are outlined below in Figure One.

Figure One: Responses to questions about acceptable standards

Standard	Range	Proposition of respondents who agreeed
When telephoning a government department with a routine request, number of minutes acceptable to wait for a representative	Not more than 2 min.	76%
	30 seconds	97%
When telephoning a government department with a routine request, number of people you should have to deal with	2 people	85%
If you leave a voice mail at 10:00, what is an acceptable time to wait for a return call?	Same day	86%
	4 hours	75 %
When you visit a government office how many minutes is it acceptable to wait in any line?	Less than 10 minutes	74%
	5 minutes	68%
When you visit a government office number of people you should have to deal with	2 people	82%
When you write to a government department, what is an acceptable time to allow for a mailed reply?	Up to 2 weeks	87%
When you e-mail a government office by 10:00 am, what is an acceptable time to wait for a reply?	4 hours	90%
	Next day not acceptable	74%

Based on this information, the CCSN has developed a checklist to guide providers through service improvement plans for telephones and information.

- How often do your clients reach a busy signal, and, if often, have you explored options to address this?

- Do you and your staff return phone messages within four hours?

- If you are unable to return phone calls within four hours, does your message explain when you will be able to return the call?

- Does your message provide clients with the option of reaching a person?

- Can citizens locate your phone number, e-mail, website and mailing address easily?

- Do your staff have access to the information they need to answer client queries?

- Are your staff trained and do they have the tools necessary to meet all the information needs of clients?

- If your staff do not have access to all information necessary to answer client questions, do they know who possesses that information so that clients are 'bounced' no more than once? (CCMD 1999, p. 9).

A checklist has also been developed for improving timeliness.

The CCSN also emphasise the need to take a holistic, government-wide approach to developing citizen-centred services, as citizens will often need to contact more than one department in order to fulfil a single service need. They have explored the use of single window services in order to achieve this (for further information see *Innovations and Good Practices in Single-Window Service,* CCSN: http://www.ccmd-ccg.gc.ca).

Research Report Series

1. *Partnership at the Organisation Level in the Public Service*, Richard Boyle, 1998
2. *The Role of Strategy Statements*, Richard Boyle and Sile Fleming, 2000
3. *Flexible working in the Public Service*, Peter C. Humphreys, Sile Fleming and Orla O'Donnell, 2000.